JIVARO

HEAD-HUNTERS OF THE AMAZON

JIVARO
HEAD-HUNTERS OF THE AMAZON
Bertrand Flornoy
ISBN 978-1-84068-188-8
Published 2012 by Creation Books
Copyright © Creation Books 2012
Introduction copyright © Jack Hunter 2011
DOCUMENTS OF CULTURE : ETHNOGRAPHY

CONTENTS

INTRODUCTION
AMAZON DEATH MAGIC

DISCOVERING THE JIVARO

The first Europeans to encounter the Shuar, or Jivaro, Indians of the Ecuador-Peru jungle were the Spanish conquistadors in the 16th century. The Jivaro were the only tribe to successfully rebel against Spanish rule; they staged a campaign of vicious warfare against their oppressors, with two successive raids in 1599 reportedly resulting in the deaths of 26,000 Spanish settlers. The Jivaro became feared for their ferocity and cruelty; those they caught were tortured, disembowelled, skinned alive, burnt, hacked to pieces. They would also sooner kill their own children than let them fall into Spanish hands.

Internecine tribal warfare was the Jivaro way of life, a constant cycle of bloody vengeance marked by a singular practice: the taking, preserving and shrinking of human heads as trophies of war. These shrunken heads, known as *tsantsas*, were said to enable warriors to control the ghosts of their slaughtered enemies, and to confer social status. As this practise of death magic suggests, the Jivaro were also shamanistic, searching for ancient spectres through the ingestion of powerful hallucinogens.

Systematic attempts at Christianizing the Jívaro were made between 1645 and 1767, but all were doomed to failure; missionaries were driven out, killed, decapitated. By the end of the 19th century, a few missionaries had returned but very little was still known about the Jivaro, except for one thing: the legend of the head-shrinkers. Fascination with this practise among Western collectors led to an emergent trade in shrunken heads as macabre works of primitive art; this trade escalated as more and more expeditions penetrated the Jivaro interior, and ethnological reports appeared in popular publications such as *National Geographic*. When the Jivaro found that they could trade the heads in exchange for guns and other items, they began to increase production, which invariably meant an escalation in warfare and slaughter. Heads bought guns, guns killed more enemies to provide even more heads, even more heads bought even more guns in a spiralling cycle which threatened to result in eventual race suicide. The Peruvian and Ecuadorean governments finally intervened in the 1920s, making the trafficking of shrunken heads illegal.

JIVARO IN POPULAR CULTURE

Published in 1953, Bertrand Flornoy's *Jivaro* was an ethnographic travelogue pitched somewhere between *National Geographic* and the lurid "men's adventure" pulps of that decade, such as *South Sea Stories*. Flornoy, at one time president of the Societé des Explorateurs et des Voyageurs Français, was the leader of numerous expeditions into the Upper Amazon, and highly honoured for his work. He produced not only books but also films, including *My Friend Ti, Head-Shrinker* (1948). Nonetheless, *Jivaro* – like many literary and cinematic ethnographs before it – cannot avoid a certain element of exploitation in its lurid descriptions (and photographs) of naked tribespeople, witchcraft, psychotropic delirium, and the murderous head-shrinking cult which is the book's primary focus and

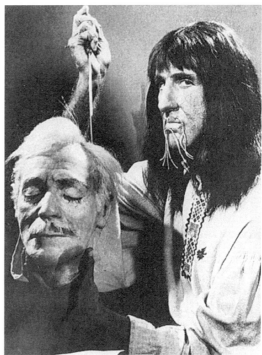

Bertrand Flornoy
                                                                    The Four Skulls Of Jonathan Drake

selling-point. As engaging as Flornoy's travelogue is, the reader is basically being set up for the grand climax – a man-hunt, decapitation, and the ritual shrinking of the harvested head. It remains a classic example of populist ethnography.

The film *Jivaro*, made by Edward Ludwig in 1954 and quite possibly inspired by Flornoy's book, is somewhat disappointing; although sub-titled *Head-Hunters Of The Amazon*, it's essentially a romantic adventure story with little in the way of massacre, decapitation or head-boiling.[1] More suitably macabre was Edward L. Cahn's *The Four Skulls Of Jonathan Drake* (1959), in which a young man discovers himself to be the victim of a curse placed upon his explorer grandfather by Jivaro Indians. With images of shrunken heads, lips sewn together, floating skulls and a headless corpse, this was Cahn's horror masterpiece and represents a peak of pulp culture's engagement with the legend of the Jivaro.[2]

By the 1960s, that engagement was also flourishing in men's adventure magazines. Lurid images of shrunken or severed heads appeared on the cover of *Sportsman*, *Men*, *Male*, and *For Men Only*, among others. Perhaps the best piece of all was published in a 1960 edition of *South Sea Stories*, and written by Jane Dolinger, a kind of ethnographer-cum-stripper whose exotic reports almost invariably included photographs of her semi-naked. Her article, entitled "I Watched A Head-Shrinking Orgy", contains a graphic account of the head-shrinking process, as well as many intriguing photographic images.

1. The only known film footage of the head-shrinking ritual as performed on a human head was shot in 1961 by explorer Edmundo Bielawski; Bielawski's documentary shows the severed head of a recently-deceased victim being boiled, processed and shrunken over a period of several days.

2. The film may have been inspired by Maurice Sandoz's short horror story "The Tsantsa" (1945).

"A strange hush fell over the Jivaros. Now all eyes were focused on the basket. The witch doctor's chant became a frenzied shriek and ended on a high discordant note. My heart pounded furiously and I tensed as I saw the tiwipa's hand snake into the open basket and bring out the bloody head. Standing, he held it high, so that all could see. It was the head of a girl – a young girl about 15 years of age. She had long blue-black hair and the color of her skin had turned a sickening white. Her eyes were closed and her pale lips were slightly parted. Dirt and coagulated blood covered the neck where it had been severed from the body."

In the 1970s, cannibalism became the vogue atrocity with a series of Italian gore movies set in the Amazon, principally Umberto Lenzi's *Cannibal Ferox*; the sinister head-shrinkers were seemingly forgotten in this anthropophagic avalanche of blood, cruelty, death and dismemberment. Perhaps now is the right time to re-examine them.

Jane shot "still life" of shrunken heads in Jivaro village in southern Ecuador. Second, third heads from left were white men. – "I Watched A Head-Shrinking Orgy"

FOREWORD
INDIAN HEAD-HUNTERS OF THE INTERIOR

ECUADOR

Ecuador is a land of great interest to the Northerner, whether he be a scientist or layman; or whether his inclinations lead him to a study of peoples, their customs and traditions, or to the enjoyment of the natural features of the country – the birds, the mammals, the magnificent forests and lofty mountains.

This republic occupies a unique geographical position, astride the Equator, where it extends approximately from one degree thirty minutes north latitude to almost 5 degrees south latitude. Within this comparative short distance are included some of the grandest of the Andean peaks and a multitude of mighty ranges and deep canyons.

On the west coast, Ecuador holds a strategic position in regard to the Humboldt Current, that chill invader from southern seas, for it is at this point that the current sheers off to the westward and its influence upon the winds and the climatic conditions of South America is weakened.

The eastern boundaries of the republic lie across Amazonian drainage, and cut the Napo, the Pastaza, and the Paute, all affluents of the world's largest river.

The topography is extremely mountainous. Although there are restricted plains in western Ecuador, the greater part of the republic lies along the Andes and their foothills, so that level areas of any great extent are seldom encountered.

The drainage of the country includes a number of large rivers flowing to the eastward, as well as several important western-flowing streams.

Except for a narrow, coastal strip, Ecuador receives abundant rainfall. The year is divided into two seasons – the dry season, and the wet or so-called rainy season. The rains generally begin in December or January and last until May or June, the balance of the year having only a scanty rainfall.

In some localities there is a deviation from this order, and on the eastern slopes of the Andes, there are heavy rains in every month of the year. The annual rainfall in some parts of the Oriente may reach as high as 150-200 inches.

ECUADOR JIVAROS ARE HEAD-HUNTING INDIANS

The population of Ecuador is made up of three distinct elements. Most of the educated, upper class are of Spanish descent and all of the political offices are filled by men of this type. The great bulk of the population, however, is Indian, the Quichuas, who are themselves the descendants of the Incas.

The third element of the Ecuadorean population comprises the wild and savage Indian tribes of the Oriente, typified by the Jivaro or head-hunters. These latter Indians, while nominally under the government of Quito, are so far removed by the inaccessibility of their home territory that Ecuadorean laws rest lightly upon them, and they are in many respects as primitive today as when America was discovered.

It is to the purely American elements of the population that one looks for strange customs of interest to the northern visitor, and the Indians do not prove disappointing in this respect.

The Indians of the Oriente are much more savage and uncivilized than their brethren of the western Andes, the Quichuas. The Jivaros come into contact with the whites only occasionally, since the country they inhabit is very inhospitable in its climate, its dense, trackless jungles, and to a certain extent in its human population as well. They live in scattered communities along the tributaries of the Rio Napo and the Rio Paute, seldom venturing very far up on the slopes of eastern Andes, but remaining below an elevation of 3,500 feet.

WARRIORS ACQUIRE THEIR WIVES AS SPOILS OF WAR

The Jivaro wage a constant warfare among themselves for which polygamy is the direct cause. We were told that when a girl arrives at the marriageable age, about 12-14 years, she is given in marriage by her father to some friend, but most of the wives are gained by the killing of an enemy and the confiscation of the women as the spoils of war. A man may have from 5-8 wives.

The warfare may be against a member of a neighbouring tribe or against a fellow Jivaro living at some distance. The women and children of the slain man are adopted into the household of the victor, where they become members of the family and are treated in the same manner as the immediate family, not as slaves.

These Indians have a pseudo-religion which is based on a belief in being called by the Spaniards, *el diablo*, the devil. He has the attributes of a super Jivaro, is all powerful in everything the under takes, but is not particularly addicted to evil for its own sake.

No important project is undertaken without first consulting *el diablo* and getting his views. The Jivaros do not appear to have a highly developed priestly class and any man may enter into consultation with him. To do this it is necessary to retire to the seclusion some spot remote from the rest of the Jivaro, and here the would-be communicant prepares himself for the ordeal by drinking a quantity of a certain extract made from a particular variety of bark. The fluid is dark, about the colour of coffee, and contains some very powerful narcotic principle, for it produces a stupor and hallucinations of a different type but in a way comparable to the result of opium or hemp.

While under the influence of this drink, which may be for 4-5 hours, the Jivaro imagines that the devil comes to him and discusses whatever matter is afoot. Inasmuch as the mind of the man is filled with his plans when he takes this narcotic, it is but natural that his disordered reason concocts a fanciful dialogue and arrives at a confirmation of what he really believed when he first came.

If the devil has properly coached his client and the raid is eminently successful, the hut of the victim is surrounded, and when the latter steps out of the door he receives at close range the contents of all the guns in the party. The women and children are hastily captured and the raiders seek the safety of their own neighborhood, with the reasonable assurance that sooner or later they will be raided in a like manner by relatives of the slain man.

PREPARING A VICTIM'S HEAD AS A LASTING TROPHY

The head of the victim is cut off, and later, in the seclusion of his hut, the victor prepares it into a lasting war trophy, attaching to it the significance which the North American attached to scalps. The skin is opened up from the base of the neck to the crown, and the skull is removed entire, leaving only the soft, pliant skin.

The skin is now dipped into a vegetable extract which dyes it a blue-black and probably has some action preservative, and then the cut skin is sewed up along the neck to restore the head to its original form.

The cavity is filled with hot sand or pebbles, after which the head is constantly turned and moved, so that the drying goes on uniformly. When the sand has cooled, hot sand takes its place, and this process may last for several days before the head is completely cured.

Shrinking to an unbelievable degree takes place, but it is so regulated that the features retain their individuality to a great extent, and the finished head is about the size of a man's fist.

The lips have been sewed shut with a series of long cotton cords, the exact pattern of this stitching varying with the locality and seeming to have some significance.

Within a short time after the preparation of a head, generally within a month, the victor celebrates the event by a ceremonial dance at which there is an orgy of wild drinking. After this dance it may be possible to buy the head from the Jivaro, if his interest can be aroused in an object whose value he understands and appreciates, such as the musket.

SOUVENIR CRAZE STIMULATED HEAD-HUNTING

Because of the interest aroused in the outside world by tales concerning these head-hunters, there has been in the past a lively trade in human heads. The Jivaros, learning that there was a demand which could be capitalized into muskets, quickly gave a ready response; so that it became necessary for the Ecuadorean Government strictly to forbid the traffic in these objects.

Tales are told of the results of this practice which are not without a certain grim irony. There is a story, for example, of a red-headed white man who went into the interior on a trip of exploration charged with the commission of bringing out a dried and shrunken head. It was months after he had departed that a shrunken-head came out, by devious channels, from the Oriente, but the head had red hair. Perhaps a red-haired head brought the price of 2 muskets; who could tell?

Contrary to our expectations, after hearing stories of the Jivaro (and to the average Ecuadorean the word *Jivaro* is synonymous with violent death and all manner of disagreeable things), we found then a good-natured people and very friendly to us.

Like the Quichuas, they are below medium height, but with a splendid chest development and with a rather pleasing cast of countenance. The men wear their hair long, but often cut it away to form bangs in front, and it is ornamented with tufts of bright red and yellow toucan feathers on the crown and the base of the neck.

The men wear slender tubes of bamboo thrust through the lobes of the ears and the women often have a short piece of cane projecting straight out from the lower lip.

FAITHLESS WIVES RECEIVE DIRE PUNISHMENT

On their own trails, the Jivaro costume could scarcely be considered a burden to the wearer, but when these Indians visit the border settlements they wear a one-piece garment consisting of a cotton cloth, which they weave themselves, caught up around the waist.

The men we saw appeared to treat their wives kindly and showed a consideration for their wishes in minor matters. If a wife is detected in any breach of infidelity, however, she is subject to a terrific course of discipline.

For the first offense the punishment consists of throwing the erring woman to the ground, holding her there, and cutting down on to the crown of her head with a large machete, or brush knife. The man makes a great many cuts, which are at an angle to one another, so that the scalp is literally hacked into small pieces and all the hair is lost.

Should this not prove sufficient to inculcate fidelity, the second offense results in the woman's being pinned to the earth by a long, iron-pointed lance, which is thrust deep into the ground through the fleshy parts of both legs. Given food, water and sufficient care to prevent death, the offender is left in this position for days, even for a period as long as three weeks. For the third offense the punishment is death outright.

BLOW-GUNS AND POISONED ARROWS ARE THE NATIVE WEAPONS

As hunters and woodsmen the Jivaros are unsurpassed. Observers of the keenest sort, endowed with that natural instinct of the savage in knowing direction, they hunt and roam over the vast unbroken stretches of jungle, following the paths made by wild animals or slipping through more open regions regardless of trails, calling monkeys down the green hillsides by wonderful imitations of their calls, and sleeping at night like beasts themselves, where darkness overtakes them.

They hunt largely with the blow-gun, in the use of which they are peculiarly adept. The missiles for these weapons, which are sometimes twelve feet or more in length, are sun-baked balls of clay for the smaller game and poisoned arrows of cane for larger animals.

The poison is apparently a form of *curare* and is obtained from traders farther down on Amazonian waters. It is very potent, death resulting in a few minutes after an animal has been struck; but it does not spoil the game for consumption.

Salt is said to be an antidote, if placed in the mouth of the stricken animal, and monkeys are sometimes taken alive in this manner, the Jivaro hurrying up to administer the panacea when the quarry falls from the limb in a stupor.

BARBASCO USED AS POISON FOR FISH

Another poison which is extensively employed by the Jivaros is *barbasco*, a jungle vine or creeper, which is put into the rivers to secure fish. A great pile of the plant is beaten up on the rocks until it is a pulp, and after the Indians have stationed themselves down-stream some of their number throw 2-3 hundred pounds of mash into the river and the fishing begins. The fish are killed and float down, belly up, to be gathered in by the Jivaros, who see them as they pass.

So potent is this juice that large streams may be poisoned by this relatively small amount of *barbasco* and under favourable circumstances fish are stricken for a distance of three miles down-stream.

FOREWORD
A NOTE ON HUMAN TROPHY HUNTING

HUMAN TROPHIES

The practice of preserving as a trophy the head or some other bodily part of an enemy killed on the field of battle or executed at home is very widespread in South America. Moreover, since the subject of trophies has seldom failed to interest ancient and modern travellers, there is ample documentation for the practice. A great variety of motives of a psychological, social, and religious order underlie the taking and preparation of such trophies. Unfortunately, our sources seldom allude to the reasons for the practice, and it is only in the case of the Jivaro that we may discern some of the implications of head hunting. Though many South American Indian tribes celebrated the taking of heads with great rejoicing and honoured those who obtained them, no tribe, not even the Jivaro, seem to have developed the institution to the same extent as have some Malayan and Papuan tribes. Among the Jivaro the possession of a trophy head seems to have ensured good luck to the owner, first because it contained *tsarutama* or magic power and secondly, because it secured the good will of the ancestors whose desire for revenge was gratified. Before its preparation, however, the head was considered to be inert and impotent; it assumed its magic powers only after it had been shrunk in accordance with strict rules.

HEAD TROPHIES

Head trophies in South America may be classified into four main types: (1) skulls, (2) mummified heads, (3) shrunken heads, or *tsantsas*, and (4) skull cups.

The number of head trophies which the Spaniards found in the Indian villages of the Cauca Valley is eloquent proof of the ferocity and the bloody character of the wars waged by these Indians. The heads hung in rows from the bamboo palisades and from the walls of temples and houses and lay in heaps on platforms on the plazas. Some heads probably were mummified because with their hair and paintings they had a lifelike appearance. The bamboo supports were pierced so that the wind blew through the holes with a mournful sound.

The tribes of Veragua, Darien and Panama also kept their villages well stocked with human heads. Even though most of the skulls which Columbus found in the huts of the Taino in the West Indies clearly were the remains of ancestors, these Indians seem to have taken the heads of their enemies. There are few references to head trophies in the Guianas, but there is little doubt that here, too, the practice was general.

Early and recent accounts alike mention head trophies among the Amazonian tribes. Among the Tupinamba, Guaranty and Omagua, the skulls of enemies were stuck on posts in front of the huts or on the palisades. The Shipaya greatly valued the skulls of their enemies and hung them in nets from the roof of the huts. The trophy heads of the Mundurucu are famous because of the skill with which they were prepared. After the brain and soft parts had been removed, they were plunged in oil and then exposed to the sun and to smoke. The empty sockets were filled with artificial eyes made of wax and cutia teeth. A carrying cord was laced through the lips.

A parallel may be established between the Mundurucu trophy heads and several specimens found by Tello at Nazca, but the method of preparation was somewhat different. In Peru the skin was peeled from the skull, which was cleansed of all organic matter, and, when the skin was perfectly cured, it was again stretched over the skull. Like the shrunken heads of the Jivaro, the Nazca trophies have skewers through the lips.

Scenes represented on the ceramics and textiles of the Nazca, lea, and Tiahuanaco Periods bear ample evidence of the importance given by these early civilizations to trophy heads. Some details suggest that the heads were perhaps shrunken like the Jivaro *tsantsas*.

The Inca celebrated their victories by parading the heads of their enemies on the tips of lances or by bringing the trophies to Cuzco.

From historical sources as well as from rock paintings and vase decorations, we know that the bellicose Diaguita took the heads of their victims. Some of the skulls have been found in tombs in the valley of Humahuaca.

The Araucanians kept only the heads of famous enemies and of the prisoners whom they killed after a victory.

SHRUNKEN HEADS

The Jivaro owe their fame to the shrunken heads, or *tsantsas*, which they still prepared in modern times and which have been eagerly sought after by collectors.

In pre-Columbian times the art of shrinking heads was widespread in the Andean area. Early chroniclers have given us excellent descriptions of shrunken heads and of the methods of their preparation among the Indians of the Ecuadorian Coast. Vases in the shape of shrunken heads and representations of heads reminiscent of the *tsantsas* may be assigned to the Nazca, lea, and Tiahuanaco Periods, but shrunken heads themselves have not been found in Peru. It is a moot question whether the countless heads with skewered lips painted on Nazca vases actually were reduced or were prepared like the specimens described by Tello.

In the 17th century, the neighbours of the Jivaro, the Maina, Ohehero, and Cocama, also prepared *tsantsas* from the heads of their enemies.

SKULL CUPS

Following an ancient custom, the Araucanians made a cup from the skull of the famous conquistador Valdivia. The same method of scorning the enemy occurred in Peru, where the skull vessels were often mounted on silver. It was also found among many tribes of the Chaco, Brazil, and the Guianas.

STUFFED CORPSES

The most spectacular trophies displayed by South American Indians were the stuffed bodies of their enemies. The Indians of the Cauca Valley seem to have carried this practice to extremes. Cieza de Leon (1932) writes that he saw in Cali on a platform, "corpses which had been opened and flayed with a flint knife and eaten. The skins were then stuffed with ashes, the faces remodeled with wax; they were set up in lifelike position." These Indians also preserved the feet and hands of their enemies and even their ash-filled intestines. The Huanca

Indians of the Valley of Xauxa similarly placed the stuffed skins of war captives in their temples. Even the Inca stuffed the corpses of war captives with ashes or straw, and made their stomachs into drums. To add to the insult, the hands of the corpse were so arranged that he seemed to be drumming on his own stomach and a flute was placed in his mouth.

The flaying of enemy corpses has been reported for the Arara, a Carib tribe of the lower Xingu River.

The ancient Quechua made drum heads of the skin of their enemies. The Araucanians made rattles from the dried skin of their enemies' hands, and at dances they wore masks made from the dried and moulded facial skin of dead captives. Occasionally, they stuffed the bodies with straw. Some of the Abipon made arrow quivers from the cured skin of their enemies' hands. Stuffed hands were seen by Sotelo de Narvaez among the Indians of Santiago del Estero in the Argentine.

SCALPING

Scalping has been reported only in two regions of South America: in the Chaco, where it was practiced by several tribes (Mataco, Toba, Pilagd, Mocovi, Ahipon, Mhayd) and in the Guianas, where it is ascribed to the Carib by several usually reliable sources. The occurrence of the custom in the Guianas is most disconcerting. Friederici (1929) tries to ascribe it to the influence of escaped North American Indians brought to the Guianas as slaves; but this hypothesis is not acceptable to Roth (1924), who believes scalping to be an indigenous practice. The Chaco Indians made cups out of the dry skin from the scalp and a portion of the face. The Toba and Ashluslay mounted their scalps on a wooden hoop. When a war party returned with scalps, festivities were organized and masked dancers jumped and ran around the poles from which the trophies were hung. Scalping also is reported among the Arara, a little-known tribe of the lower Xingu River. They took not only the scalp, but also the ears and mounted the trophy on a hoop (Nimuendaju, 1924).

BONE TROPHIES

In countless South American tribes from the Guianas to Chile, the bones of dead enemies were made into arrow heads or flutes. The Araucanians cut off the arms and legs of dead war prisoners and made flutes of the long bones to celebrate their triumph. The Turuna made trumpet bells out of skulls. The trophies most commonly mentioned among the Indians of Santa Marta, Colombia, Venezuela, the Guianas, Brazil, and Paraguay are tooth necklaces. These ornaments have been reported also in the Pampas, but not in Peru; perforated human teeth, however, were found archeologically on the Coast. Among the ancient Guarani, old women made necklaces out of the teeth of the victims of cannibalistic feasts. Mundurucu warriors who had fought bravely but, because of a wound, had failed to obtain a head, were compensated with the gift of a cotton belt from which hung the teeth removed from enemy heads. Such a belt might also be given to the widow of a warrior killed in battle; its possession entitled her to community support.

JIVARO

HEAD-HUNTERS OF THE AMAZON

BERTRAND FLORNOY

TABLE OF PHOTOGRAPHS

PART ONE : SEARCHING

ONE : THE ADVENTURE BEGINS

I

The region of the upper Amazon lies between two and five degrees Latitude South and 74 and 79 degrees Longitude West. It is a land of deep forests pitted with lagoons and laced by rivers – a vast green marshland where the sun never shines. Treasure, a vast hidden store of oil and gold, rubber and copper, lies there awaiting discovery, but the men who seek it leave no trace. Man cuts his way in, armed with all the weapons of the moderns, and the forest closes the paths behind him between one dawn and the next. In this green gloom there are no echoes, no comforting animal cries; only the steaming heat and the insects and the unending forest.

The forest defeated the Incas, the first civilized people who tried to conquer it. Six captains of the Children of the Sun reached the eastern slope of the Cordillera of the Andes. At much the same time, Huayna-Capac sailed down the Rio Chinchipe from the south and attempted to trace the tortuous course of the Marañon river. Both expeditions met first the forest and then the Indians. Poisoned arrows slew them and the nameless swamps swallowed their remains.

After them, for 100 years the Amazon was left in peace. Then came the Spaniards, armed and booted and surrounded by an army of dogs and pigs and hill Indians. Among them were the adventurers Gonzalo Pizarro, Orelana, and Juan de Salinas, who left the shores of the Pacific to seek cinnamon and the Golden King of the Incas, and found themselves, one day, on the shores of the Atlantic.

These expeditions did no more than skirt the Upper Amazon, but as they passed, the Rio Napo, the Rio Santiago and the Marañon were traced on the first hesitant maps as navigable rivers. Settlements were established on the edge of the forest and the western part of the country was divided into four provinces "to be subdued". While Philip III ruled over the Spanish Empire, villages were built at great cost in human life: villages with Spanish names like Logrono, Mcndoza, Sevilla de Oro and Borjo.

But one day, from the forest close by the walls, 20,000 Indians, frenzied rather than ferocious, rushed forth to attack the threatening invaders. Everything was destroyed: the villages were burned, the men slaughtered, only the nuns escaped with their lives to seek refuge in distant huts. Legend has it that at Logrono the Spanish Governor was forced to drink molten gold.

This crushing defeat exhausted the zeal of the conquerors, but not the faith of the missionaries. In the steps of Inca and Spaniard came the Jesuits, the Passionites and the Dominicans to carry Cross and compass deep into the forest. Tribes which had not yielded to violence knelt before the Indian Christ borne in the hands of these lean proselytes. Today their heroism can be found recorded in books; but the forest has concealed every trace of them.

Years later the white man came again, this time in search of rubber. In the hastily built village of Iquitos, deep in the forest, the echoes of Viennese waltzes and the naïve extravaganzas of the 'nineties could be heard. Strolling players from the casts of operettas from overseas, overwhelmed by the steamy heat, rubbed shoulders in the muddy streets with the first civilized Indians – Indians with faces painted with magical designs. In the hinterland the repeating rifle brought destruction to the Indians. But it did not last. The boldest pioneers succumbed to fever or to Indian arrows and the slump in rubber drove the survivors home.

Next came the scientists, among them Doctor Rafael Carsten who lost an eye working in the cause of science among the Indians of Eastern Ecuador and on the right bank of the Marañon. Finally, in our own day, the Peruvians, reviving the dream of their Inca ancestors, came down from the skies in hydroplanes, adorned with red and white emblems, and landed on the great lonely rivers.

Yet the upper Amazon, goal of so many quests, remains largely unknown, a still legendary region. The natives who inhabit it defended their domain river by river. The white man's relations with these tribes – the Cocoma, the Zapparo, the Murato, the Shappra – have gratified his pride but given him little else. Faithful to their ancient traditions they have accepted with indifference the commercialized civilization that offers them God between two remnants of cloth. They have kept their liberty though they have often paid for a pair of trousers with its weight in gold.

But one tribe has made no concessions at all. The Jivaros, crueller than their neighbours, have obstinately refused to betray their proud past. Racially pure, they still lead their semi-nomadic life in the heart of the upper Amazon. They dwell today scattered in small communities on the right and left banks of the Marañon, or else forced northwards into the unhealthiest districts and amid torrential rivers.

Head-hunting and head-shrinking are still practised by them. Their fame is acknowledged among all who have met them. But it is a fame that has erected a barrier of fear between the people in the populated districts outside the Amazon and the Jivaros themselves.

And this was the people we wanted to visit.

II

We were nobody's idea of the intrepid explorers of romantic fiction. The journalists who interviewed us first in Paris and then on board the steamship *Alaska*, in port at Antwerp, were plainly astonished that three such men should wish to go in search of the hidden secrets of the Amazon and, in particular, the habits and life of the head-shrinkers.

Our combined ages totalled only 77 years. We had come together, believing in adventure, in danger, in the joy of discovery, one from the snows, a second from the desert and the third – myself – from the virgin forest. My companions were Fred Matter, the party's cinephotographer. He was slightly the oldest, a tough, stubborn Alsatian with a soft heart who had just returned from the french expedition among the ice and snow of Eastern Greenland.

The youngest was Jean de Guébriant, a fair-haired, spectacled Breton, calm and precise, who had recently completed the first round-the-Mediterranean motor trip. Jean was in charge of the geographical side. I was the party's ethnographer.

We had the official blessing of the Ministry of National Education and the Geographical Society of France, and the good wishes of a great many laboratories, public men and personal friends. They sent us on our way with a great deal of valuable material and moral aid. On the eve of our departure from Quito, the Ecuadorean capital, into the forests of the Amazon, we received a letter from Commandant Charcot in which he said: "Do sound work. Go at it fearlessly. Bring back something worth while."

TWO : GATEWAY TO THE AMAZON

I

The *Alaska* delivered us to Guayaquil, principal port of the Republic of Ecuador and the first step of our journey. The town spread out in front of us, flat, dazzlingly white, unmysterious, a colonial city bare of monuments despite its four centuries of history. The original city, the work of the great Benalcazar, was sacked by a succession of enemies: by Francis Drake, said to be a sadist and a dandy; by Morgan the incendiary; by the Dutch pirates of 1624 who raped the women and, for the sake of hygiene, burned everyone else; by bands of Frenchmen, later on by Spanish Jews, and finally by pestilence.

Guayaquil sprawls over the right bank of the river Guayas; the train for Quito, the capital, leaves from the left bank. Matter, Guébriant and I mingled with the sleepy crowd going on board the formidable paddle-steamer, which transports passengers and baggage higgledy-piggledy over the Guayas, as it lay at the landing stage, hooting gently.

The grey dawn rang with the cries of the women selling maize cakes and meat cakes: "*dos reales cado uno... dos.*"

Yellow-faced boys were selling *L' Universo*, from which our three photographs smiled farewell. A negro, leering like a pimp, proffered razor-blades.

When all the travellers were installed in the bowels of the old steamer, the chains were loosed. The current was strong, and while the steamer manoeuvred among launches and boats we had time to stare at our companions. We saw a host of solemn faces; one hook-nosed old woman chatting to a handsome green and yellow parrot; planters and their families; small tradesmen endlessly counting their fibre suitcases.

Ticket-collectors, as strict as sergeant-majors, questioned us, while out in midstream an Indian canoe sailed past, loaded with pineapples and parakeets. When the steamer touched the landing-stage on the opposite bank there was a rush for the narrow-gauge train. It seemed likely to collapse under the pressure of the crowd, and yet it was to take us all the way to the capital over mountain passes more than 13,000 feet high.

As the train climbed higher the increasing cold seemed to affect landscape as well as travellers for it shed its lush vegetation while we piled on more wraps. Trees grew sparse, ferns dwindled; there were no more flowers, only pale *agaves* thrusting out of the soil. We met the first Cordillera Indians, inscrutable-faced, clad in long red and black ponchos or thick sheepskin trousers. They watched us pass without a gesture, as unmoved by our presence as were their fathers by the Spanish horsemen or as their children will be by four-engined airliners.

Thirteen thousand feet up, we halted on the *paramo*, a high, cinder-covered plateau. Except for the bustle and clatter of the train, we were alone with the overwhelmingly melancholy grey sky. The mountains, to our relief, were neighbours now, no longer arrogant. Then we began the descent; in the late afternoon we passed through cultivated land and well-marked fields until we reached Riobambas, hub of Ecuador, where we stayed the night. Next day we reached the capital.

II

It was in Quito that we made our first acquaintance with the handiwork of the Jivaros. We paid an official visit to the French Minister, a sturdy bearded man who gave, us wise advice, for he had travelled as far as Baños, the last village before the forest. But he had something to show us that was better than good advice. On the first floor of the Legation, in a room crammed full of Indian lances, blow-guns, necklaces and feathered ornaments, we had our first sight of a shrunken human head.

In fact there were 30 of them. They stood before us, a weird and extraordinary collection in 30 square cardboard boxes. Each head was no bigger than a man's fist, reduced to the size of an orange by an ancient, complicated and skilful craft which we were one day to see performed.

Not all these trophies were the genuine work of the Jivaros. For some years the mass production of shrunken heads had been going on for the benefit of the tourist trade. A few Indians, caught by commerce, have discovered how to take advantage of their macabre skill; and an organization which functions between a tiny village in the South and the capital itself has discovered how to take advantage of the Indians. For the price of a few yards of white cloth the Indian will dig up a corpse and shrink its head according to the technique consecrated by their ancestors. Then a half-caste passes it over to an agent in Pinto – perhaps a hotel porter or a bazaar owner – until today there are few tourists who have not handled one of these extraordinary trophies.

How can you tell an authentic *tsantsa* (the native word for the shrunken head) from an imitation? Only by subtle details: the length of the hair, the degree of delicacy of the scars and stitches at the back of the head, the absence or presence of lip ornaments. The forgers have no magic or religious tradition to maintain and their work betrays it.

The heads were shown to us as a warning of the dangers of venturing into the Jivaro country and to try and make us realize our folly in risking our lives for what our friends thought was the silly object of gaining a few scraps of information about the habits of the tribe. We were not deterred, not even by the most terrifying story of them all. It was told to us by a monk who had no intention of trying to dissuade us from our journey. He had once been a missionary. Now he was ravaged by fever though he concealed his agony under a great kindness, and we heard the tale as we sat with him in the stillness of a beautiful cloister garden.

It happened, he said, during the time of the great uprisings, when Ecuador, intoxicated by its new-found freedom, was in full revolutionary fever. The Battle of the Constitutions was being waged at Ambato and Quito; at Guayaquil they were hanging generals from the lamp-posts; many Indians were massacred and monks were jailed. But among the monks was one Jesuit who, told that he must be deported, chose for his exile not the country of his birth but the lands of the Amazon which on old maps were left blank except for the comment: "Little known regions inhabited by savage Indians."

At first, as he travelled on the desolate upland plateaux of the Cordillera, he met only sympathy and kindness. The Indians in their woollen cloaks knelt to him in supplication as he passed.

Later, when he went down to the region of rushing rivers east of the Andes, he met the hostile tribes that turn away the stranger from their firesides. The forest closed up behind him; but between the Santiago and the Morona rivers he found the people he was seeking: the Jivaros.

We do not know how he managed to win their friendliness, but at first he was allowed to live in their midst baptizing and healing. No doubt he was given food and a folding bed of bamboo in every hut he visited, for "uncivilized" Indians sympathize with the destitute. But his time of peace did not last long. His piety, and ministrations to the sick drew down upon him the wrath of the most powerful man in the community, the witch-doctor. In a sacred frenzy, drunk with *natema*, the witch-doctor denounced him and he was murdered.

Then, in savage passion, the Indians shrivelled not merely his head, but *his whole body*. Years afterwards a traveller in Southern regions, seeking salt, saw in a hut in the Upper Morona a blackened corpse, no bigger than a child's, hanging near the bed of a warrior while the warrior himself, clad majestically in a large cassock, sat on a stool drinking fermented *yamanche*.

III

In Quito we made our final preparations.

We planned to reach the forest in easy stages. From Quito we intended to go to Baños, gateway to the Amazon, and from there across the plain to the *pueblo* of Puyo where the Dominican priests have built a large mission, and a Brazilian sugar-planter has his *hacienda*, called Zulay. On the way we intended to rest first at the *pueblo* of Rio Verde and then at the *hacienda* of Nunchi. From Puyo we would cross the Andean Cordillera of Sihuin on the way to Canelos, the last village on the plain. All this part of the journey would be overland, but after Canelos we should have to take to the rivers of the Amazon and begin our search for the Jivaros by scouring the banks of the tributaries of the Rio Pastaza.

For the journey we needed a guide and mules to transport our extensive baggage and equipment as far as Canelos. There the mules could be left behind and we would have to engage canoes and canoeists – if we could find any brave enough to venture among "the heathen".

Our search for a competent guide was answered by the arrival of Ramon Olalla, a taxidermist well known in the museums of Europe and America. He introduced himself one morning, together with his references and a wonderful collection of humming birds beautifully prepared and labelled. We approved of him. Moreover, we found him mentioned in terms of the highest praise in Chapman's handbook.

Ramon could speak Kitchua and, so he said (which w afterwards found to be untrue), Jivaro. That evening we decided to engage him and he helped us to prepare our cases. Our equipment was taken out of the packing cases which had held it since we left Paris, divided into parcels weighing between 80 and 90 pounds each – as much as a single porter could carry – then covered with waterproof cloth and packed up again in 56 cases.

The equipment of the expedition, the choice of stores and medical supplies, had been the result of much anxious thought. We were going into the interior of an inhospitable country into a warm, damp climate among dangerous fauna; a country which provides only the minimum means of subsistence and no help from the native population. Therefore we had in our 6 cases a great store of varied supplies.

The medical supplies consisted of the ordinary contents of a field medicine chest plus 8,000 pills of quinine sulphate, 160 phials for intra-muscular injection, 200 phials of emetine andacetylarsan, 24 phials of antiophidic serum from the Institut Pasteur and the Institut Vital of Brazil, phials of anti-gangrene serum, five boxes of stevarsol tablets, a set of phials of camphorated oil, caffeine and ergotin, 60 flasks of parasitol, a set of dentist's instruments and a complete surgical outfit.

Each individual's equipment consisted of: a syringe holding ten cubic centimetres, two phials of anti-toxic serum, 40 tablets of quinine and three flasks, one of tincture of iodine, one of oil of citronella and one of brandy.

The food we carried comprised 900 tins of various foods including flaked oats, compressed foods, energizing foods, powdered milk, 400 lb. of concentrated bread, 220 lb. of sugar, 220 lb. of rice, 220 lb. of manioc flour, 110 lb. of salt, powdered chocolate, tea and filter.

Among our other stores were specially-prepared batteries with a capacity of 1,500 hours of electric light; 40 gallons of petrol; a hurricane lamp; cooking utensils; tools for use in camp-construction, forestry and soldering; three-quarters of a mile of blue and white cloth; knives, mirrors, needles and thread for paying canoeists and porters and for bartering with the Indians, and four camp beds.

Besides the apparatus essential to our studies, all of which, from a compass to a set of anthropologist's tools, we kept within reach, we took two cameras, 10,000 feet of cinematographic film, 220 rolls of photographic film, a sound-recording machine and 60 discs.

Our weapons consisted of two repeating rifles (one 10 by .45), two sporting guns, three automatic pistols, 3,000 cartridges and bullets and (for fishing only!) a load of dynamite.

To give us a little pleasure we carried a gramophone and records, some books, and plenty of tobacco, cigarettes, and matches.

The total equipment weighed more than 4,500 lb., divided into 50 cases and six parcels, plus three bags of waterproof canvas for personal belongings. These could be inflated to float in case of an accident on the rivers. Finally three more waterproof bags con sleeping-bags and mosquito nets.

It is not the easiest of tasks, as we were to find out, to transport two tons of objects through the densest forest in the world.

IV

We sent off our final cables home to France, paid the last courtesy visits, completed our medical supplies, nailed up and numbered our cases and completed the inventory – even Fred Matter's harmonica was safely tucked away. Our official papers were folded in my wallet. Our well-greased firearms were dry in their waterproof covers. We were ready.

Because of a threat of landslides it was decided that we should not all go to Baños at once, but that I should travel ahead first with 20 cases and that Matter, Guébriant and Olalla should follow me 24 hours later with the rest of the freight. I made the journey without hindrance and arrived safely at Baños, a poor village ruled by a political lieutenant – something between a dictator and a police inspector – and a few sickly-faced soldiers.

Baños has no other reason for existence but its position at the mouth of a mist-filled gorge to the east, the only exit towards the forest and the distant Amazon river. It is thanks to this outlet that Baños can claim to be the gateway to adventure, but Baños is not an adventurous looking-place.

It lies in a land of water; cascades and rainstorms pour over it and drown it and the sun passes too quickly from one mountain slope to the other to allow time to dry the wretched, waterlogged walls. The natives, their decrepit frames clad in woollen *ponchos* – red with black stripes – answered my questions in a mixture of Kitchua and Spanish. Their wan faces were sad and they persisted in bowing low to me as they passed as though I had a whip in my hand.

I watched them eating in their isolated huts, enfolded and pervaded by the warm friendly gloom of a thick cloud of smoke. The men were sucking up the two traditional soups: salt (*sopa de sal*) and sweet (*sopa dolce*). When you let them eat in peace they glance at you with infinite gratitude and the women offer you a bowlful. On market days, out in the open square, they buy a mixture of meat, maize and manioc, seasoned with a formidable sort of pimento called *Aji*. Their one luxury is to get drunk on cane spirit.

As I waited for the rest of the party, strolling under a stormy sky along a path leading to a stream, a bare-footed child ran after me calling shrilly: "Boss! Boss! *Hay un derrumbe en el camino*." ("There is a landslide on the Baños road.")

Hurriedly I climbed back to the village. The political lieutenant confirmed the news. It was an avalanche of stones three miles away. The road was blocked. Somewhere behind it were my friends and the rest of our equipment.

The political lieutenant betrayed no surprise. Landslides are frequent in this unstable upland region. The eroding water soddens the thin layers of clay and betrays whole sections of the mountainside so that everything suddenly collapses with a rush and a roar. When the cloud of earth has subsided the landscape has assumed an unfamiliar shape, its contours less sharply defined, the houses of mud and reeds, torn up and drenched, are once more no longer places of habitation but simply piles of mud and reeds. Families of migrant Indians can be seen hurrying by with bowed backs, seeking a way out.

Angry with frustration I stormed at the political lieutenant as he slouched in his gloomy room before an audience of whining women and resigned policemen. He had to get moving, I told him. The rest of our expedition was on its way. I wanted men and tools to shift the stones and allow my friends to get through. I needed action today, now, this minute.

Today? His fat, coffee-coloured face widened in a broad smile. "*Mañana*," he said. "*Mañana*." Tomorrow, tomorrow – that favourite South American word which really means "In a month, perhaps."

I showed him my official papers. I pointed out the signature of the Minister of the Interior, his boss. I threatened him with dire penalties and at last, regretfully, he agreed to engage some Indians, if any could be found willing to take the job on.

We went outside. A score of Indians were sitting on the steps of the buildings in the Square, apathetically hunting lice. We offered them money and the magic word roused the poor wretches into activity. Policemen handed out spades, pickaxes and stakes. I requisitioned a lorry and the 20 men and we drove off in the rain.

The avalanche had occurred at a dangerous corner between two bends in the road where the mountain ran down to the river Baños in one sheer slope. No ridge, no rock hid the summit from our view and stones and lumps of earth were still falling. The road itself was blocked for 60 yards and we had only four or five hours in front of us before darkness.

A half-caste passed on my orders to the Indians in Kitchua. First the big blocks of stone must be pushed off the road down the slope towards the river, then a passage wide enough to admit our expedition's lorry must be dug out of the smaller stones and the sodden earth.

They went to work; but not for them were the splendid efforts of road builders, the proud gesture of uplifted arms, the ringing echo of pickaxes against rock. These Indians were indeed children of an oppressed race. They did not attack the earth, they could only displace it timidly. They were no longer threatened by Incas or Spaniards or Colonials with whips, yet they tackled the job with little meek digs.

I swore, I cursed, I stormed, using the edge of my tongue as, once, impatient Conquistadors had let fly with whips.

Work had scarcely begun when the boy who had been posted as watchman screamed a warning.

Another fall of stones skimmed past us and in the general scramble to escape one man was cruelly gashed on the leg. As he sprawled bleeding on the ground everybody looked at me. Surely now the boss would understand that nothing could be done; not today at any rate, but *mañana*, *mañana*. I drove them back relentlessly. Unwillingly they returned to their feeble efforts.

Slowly the hours passed, gradually the worst of the blockage was shifted and a passage began to appear.

Towards the end of the afternoon a sinister wrenching noise turned our eyes to the mountain top. A fresh avalanche was rolling down towards us. We ran for shelter and, from the safety of a rock, I watched the four hours' toil of those 20 men undone in a few seconds. Irrationally I thought angrily of the fat political lieutenant sitting comfortably in the public room and, no doubt, shaking his head over the antics of the impatient foreigner and murmuring to himself: "*Mañana*, *Mañana*."

V

Night was falling when, turning a corner, Guébriant and Matter met the piled-up mass of earth still shuddering under the impact of the rapidly falling stones. Hastily they backed the heavy lorry some 100 yards into the shelter of a rock and then, against the plaintive advice of a *poncho*-clad native family which was squatted fatalistically by the side of the road, my two companions climbed across the heap of earth and stones to join me on the other side.

At supper that evening we celebrated the joy of finding ourselves safe and sound.

THREE : ACROSS THE AMAZONIAN PLAIN

I

It was 14 days before we were able to leave Baños on 1the next stage of the journey towards the Amazonian plain and the Dominican mission of Puyo. First we had to clear the road to get the lorry through, a tedious, miserable job which took so long that we were all surprised when it was eventually accomplished. Then we had to await the arrival of the 30 mules we had ordered from Puyo, the animals which were to carry our equipment across mountains and through forests where no vehicle could pass.

During those 14 days it rained. It rained steadily, remorselessly, without breaking or ease. I had been so cold for so long, so accustomed to feeling the waters soak into my body or watching it steam off me in a warm cloud beside a camp fire, that I had become a sort of aquatic animal. It no longer seemed sensible to dress. I resented making the absurd gestures of pulling on my icy *poncho* and my heavy boots for as soon as I left shelter the rain overwhelmed me again.

At last the mules arrived, but of the 30 we had expected only 15 had got through and they were in a dreadful state. The muleteers, led by a man called Ayala, were no better. They were covered in mud to the eyes and had no sooner reached Baños than they collapsed from exhaustion begging for a day's rest. When it was granted, they lay down on the bare ground in an open barn which usually served as a stable for their beasts and slept as though they were dead. As we watched them, these young, tough men who are kin to the *gauchos* of the pampas, we glimpsed something of the terrible ordeal that lay ahead for us.

Next day, somewhat recovered, half the mules and half our equipment, together with Guébriant, Matter and Olalla, set off towards Puyo. They climbed on their mules, dressed in rubberized headgear and waterproof cloaks that covered them down to their boots, and at their signal the procession moved slowly forward on the path down the gorge overlooking the Rio Baños. They had not gone 30 yards before they were lost to us in the rain.

Next day, when it was my turn to resume the journey with the remainder of our equipment, it was raining harder than ever. I went forward, blinded, in the narrow gorge where water oozed from the flank of every mountain, and in a dozen steps I was covered with mud. The muleteers were waiting for me in silence in the barn where they had spent the night. The mules were loaded and as I gave the last inspection I wondered anxiously whether the waterproof *tapas* (a sort of tarpaulin) would be efficient enough to prevent the rain ruining our equipment.

Still in silence we began the jogging journey. In minutes, Baños was behind us and we were in the middle of the loneliness, the utter loneliness, of the Andean Cordillera. Here, hemmed in by trees and clay and water, the mind became stagnant. Plans were unthinkable, memories impossible. The jogging step of the mule, combined with the bitter cold, produced a supremely numbing effect. The only sensation was the pleasant warmth as I swallowed the drops of water that trickled into my mouth.

How long we had been moving, how far we had travelled, I did not know; but suddenly I was roused from my inertia by shouts from the muleteers in front. I peered ahead with difficulty. One hundred yards ahead of us an enormous avalanche blocked the road, and earth was still slowly sliding down from the summit to the torrent at the bottom of the ravine.

Ayala looked impassively at the heap of earth and stones and merely said: "There wasn't anything yesterday." Then he led off his men to unload the animals.

For three hours we toiled to lay down stones to try and consolidate the shifting soil before we could begin the crossing. I went first, on foot, my hand on my mule's bridle. When you are up to your waist in mud it is difficult to say whether the mule is helping you, or you are helping your mule. All you know is that a false step can be fatal and that it is wiser not to look down. Behind us came the rest of the animals, unloaded, and the muleteers carrying the cases.

When we reached Rio Verde, a *pueblo* of some ten homes, night had already fallen. In the whole of that dismal day we had covered only five miles. The lighted windows of the Adrian hut, used by the engineers in charge of the upkeep of the Oriente Road, tempted me as a place of shelter, and I knocked. The door opened a crack, only to shut brutally in my face. As I walked away I realized that I must have looked a dirty and disgusting sight.

My muleteers were sitting in a miserable shack devouring soup. They made room for me beside a dying fire and handed me a welcome bowlful of the warm liquid. As I drank, the water ran off my face into the bowl.

Ayala advised me to thicken the soup with a sprinkling of flour; that way, after three mouthfuls, you feel full.

My meal done I sat and watched Ayala by the light of a candle. His fine face was lined by years of ordeal, but his clear, calm eyes were those of a born leader of men. Even in this gloomy hut, exhausted by the day's struggle, he was still the master of his muleteers, attentive and just. He argued the price of every bowlful of soup – one *real*, a penny! When I offered him cigarettes and my cognac flask to drain, he pulled out his own cigarettes to give me. He spoke Spanish in a grave voice that caused a hush to fall on the gathering. He told me stories of his work, a real man's work. One name he mentioned set all his listeners laughing: that of a big, tough Russian who had lived among them four or five years ago, and who had spent all his pay on chunks of meat. He was too hungry, he could not stay the course.

And then to sleep! The *iglesia*, the church, a huge unfinished barn in which we had stacked the cases, served as a shelter to Indian wanderers or families deprived of their hut by some avalanche.

There I set up the camp bed. A fire of damp branches filled the church with acrid smoke but warmed nobody. Nobody cared. We craved only sleep.

An old woman offered me her shawl and then disappeared without waiting for thanks. Around me, the *arrieros* handed one another the candle and tended their feet before going to sleep.

II

At dawn, I struggled into my soaking clothes again. It was still raining. The cases were soon collected and the procession set off. The first obstacle soon appeared: a deep torrent in full spate, which had to be crossed by means of a primitive bridge consisting of two tree-trunks covered with clay.

The first mules crossed quietly, but the sixth brought disaster. It broke into an untimely gallop and one of the two beams, rotten at the core, split under its weight. The remaining nine animals had to be pulled from one side to the other by means of a to-and-fro system of ropes while the freight was carried across the single trunk on men's backs.

Five hundred yards further on we met another landslide. This time it was right under our feet. Without warning the earth moved. Great slabs of soil began to shift towards the river. Whole trees, uprooted, clinging to the clay, crashed to their doom. A frenzy seized us. The younger muleteers, paralysed by the cold and the rain, held out their hands helplessly. Ayala alone kept his courage firm and aroused us all to struggle. He leapt ahead, shouting to his men to drive the mules to firm ground. They responded with yells and blows and one by one the terrified animals, struggling in the shifting mud, reached the safety of the road. Only the last failed. In spite of the shouts and the stones hurled ruthlessly at it, the beast let itself be carried away. But as it was slipping faster and faster, helpless, towards the stream, the men, by some miracle, managed to rescue its precious load.

Five hours later, weary, our gestures automatic, the party had crossed with no other loss than that one mule. In safety again, Ayala and his muleteers regrouped the convoy and we moved slowly forward. Nobody had eaten since the previous day but no one grumbled.

At ten o'clock that evening, just as the sky at last cast off its clouds and revealed the magnificent starry night, we reached our resting-place, the *hacienda* of Nunchi. It had taken 16 hours to cover less than 13 miles.

III

Next day I saw the sun for the first time for 16 days. As I watched it climb swiftly up an utterly blue sky I forgot the trials of our journey in the contemplation of its beauty. It showed up the low hills that formed the background to a wide landscape in which the alternately light and dark tints of tropic vegetation could already be distinguished. The stifling odour of slimy earth had gone and there were scents in the air. Birds, their wings outlined sharply against the sky, flew in groups towards the tall forest trees.

Our path on this last stage of the journey to Puyo ran for some time alongside the Baños river – or perhaps it was already the Pastaza river; it is difficult to say where the two torrents meet – and whose turbulent yellow waters struck a menacing note amid the peaceful landscape. Waterfalls and *quebradas* – branches of rivers – forced us to climb high up the mountain in search of a road for the mules and thus our path turned and twisted, now drawing near the river, now moving away from it, although its muffled roar was with us all the time.

At the *pueblo* of Mera, on a plateau baked brown by the noonday sun, we saw the Pastaza, unmistakable now, flowing wide and smooth over a bed of pebbles until, after two wide curves, it lost itself in the forest on its unknown journey through inhospitable regions where, in 20 days, we were to meet it again.

Two hours later our convoy stopped at the Dominican mission of Puyo and Guébriant and Matter came to meet me with outstretched hands.

IV

Puyo, a village of eight homes, lies between the Pindo and Puyo rivers. The mission is a tribute to the optimism of the Dominican missionaries for, taking a chance on raising a congregation in this deserted region, they built a dwelling far too large for the bamboo bed, the table and the bench which are all its furniture. Alongside the main structure stands the little chapel, resisting as best it can the attacks of a myriad of devouring insects. It contains all the appurtenances necessary for divine service: an altar, candles, an attractive statue of Christ from some native holy-image shop, even a bell. But there are more weeds than worshippers.

The other huts, scattered over a square of bare sunbaked ground, house half-caste families of uncertain occupation. Most of them had originally come there in search of gold; now they had sunk to a primitive squalor. The forest, the real forest of the Amazon, surrounds them. The snow-covered peak of the volcano of Sangay rises above them to the sky. The forest's powerful spell, its cruel watchfulness, oppresses the inhabitants; Sangay terrifies them. They say it is the abode of evil spirits, but the Dominican missionary who pointed it out to us gazed at it with warm friendliness as though it were in his confidence.

A few miles away is the *hacienda* of Zulay, an oasis of civilization which exists for the sugar cane plantations owned by a Brazilian and managed by four young colonials. Here, for a few days, we forgot our ordeals in tasting the sheer joy of civilized life: the delicious pleasure of sitting together on the veranda chatting and drinking *café au lait*, riding along the solitary path that runs downhill to the Puyo Mission, bathing in the ice-cold Pindo which flows clear and tranquil through the plantations, walking through the fields of sugar cane, idling deliciously during siesta hours listening to old French gramophone records. The four colonials who welcomed us with such charming forthrightness might easily have been airmen, sailors, diplomats or bank managers. Instead they had chosen to live on the fringe of the Amazon as we had chosen to explore it.

But there was one important difference between them and us. Each evening, before imprisoning themselves within their mosquito nets, they religiously totted up their accounts. We religiously took note of the temperature.

<h1 style="text-align:center">V</h1>

For a few days we rested at Zulay and then we began our attack on the Cordillera of Sihuin, a range which stands apart from the main western chain and reaches no great height but presents a difficult obstacle because of its thick covering of forest. There is only one way through: a warpath, 22 miles long, traced in a wavering line across valleys and ravines and so narrow that the slightest deviation is fatal.

At Puyo we said goodbye to Ayala, his men and the mules: for the next stage, until we reached Canelos, our pack-horses were Indian porters. Ramon had chosen them from among the strongest men in the Canelos tribe: 56 dark-skinned men with thick black hair and sturdy, naked bodies who awaited us with their loads in the bamboo hut used as a relay station at Indillama, at the foot of the Cordillera.

When we emerged from the dense plantation of banana trees surrounding the bamboo hut, night was already falling. We carried our beds and mosquito nets into the hut's two rooms in darkness. The beams of our electric lamps would have brought out from the walls a horde of insects, spiders, cockroaches, centipedes and mosquitoes. Even without the light we had to wage war against them with towels and slippers before we felt it safe to turn in. As we lay down it began to rain. We could hear it drumming with a steadily increasing intensity on the wide leaves of the plantains. At midnight the storm broke; at five o'clock, after a sleepless night, we all pretended to wake up and an hour later I gave the order to set off.

Day broke with difficulty through a heavy, cold mist. The naked porters, the cases fixed on their backs with long broad lianas bound across their foreheads, moved easily along the muddy path. For us, encumbered with waterproofs and boots, walking was a torment. The porters, straggling in single file along the rising path, soon found their marching rhythm, each moving according to his strength and the weight of his burden. To them the forest was a friend; it helped them as they walked. A root served to support their broad feet, a liana held out a helping hand.

But I, advancing into unknown country, was straining. My heavy boots cleared a way for me along the path, but the effort of pulling them from the heavy clay left me breathless. What should have been easy walking was a struggle and the struggle soon became a farce. If I watched the roots the lianas tore off my cap; if I watched the lianas the roots tripped me up. Behind my back the Indians were laughing silently.

Towards 11 o'clock the porters halted at the edge of a stream. Immediately they rummaged in the nearby trees and sought out their store of masticated manioc. Like the Eskimos, who cache food at intervals across the hundreds of miles of snow-covered wastes, these Indians conceal manioc in trees along the route on which they have later to return.

I watched them drinking. Each man seized a handful of *masato*, dipped it into his calabash, diluted it with water and solemnly prepared to drink. Holding the vessel with both hands, each man bent his head, put his lips to the calabash and sipped tiny mouthfuls of the whitish liquid from which they draw all their strength, all their powers of endurance. They performed the rite gravely; Indians never smile while drinking their *masato*.

But when the beverage was drunk and their stomachs were full the porters were in good humour. They allowed us to take their photographs. They felt our boots, they even tried on Guébriant's cap. As they did so a little sunlight filtered through the thick blanket of leaves, giving us fresh courage to resume the march.

In the evening, after countless efforts and tumbles, we reached a series of river branches. Too weary to take off our boots we forded the river with the water up to mid-thigh and then, because we enjoyed it, up to the neck. On land again we went on in the steaming heat, counting the minutes, until at last, from a final hillock, we saw the Bobonaza River. One loop of it was gleaming in the setting sun and, nestling in the land which it bordered, we saw the elliptical roofs of Indian huts glowing cheerfully as spots of red-brown against the green of the forest. We had reached the mission of Canelos.

VI

Canelos, the last village before the forest, shines with a rare radiance amid the green immensity of the Amazon. The actual village consists of a single square containing the monastery, its chapel and two houses on pile foundations, one of which stands empty while in the other lives the political lieutenant, and a few huts.

The Canelos are a peaceful tribe. Down the years they have accepted and absorbed the nomadic tribes of Indian families who have drifted there by stages from Napol, from the Tigre, from the Curaray and from the Pastaza. Civilization, through the humanizing medium of the monks, has brought them a few aids to happiness: they have acquired cloth, the woodcutter's axe, the *asuela* – a tool for hollowing out canoes – a few medicines and the word of God.

Today God appears in the shape of Father Leon, a man of sensitive face, white beard and splendid smile. Forty-five of his 75 years have been spent in missionary work among the Indians, as priest, doctor and schoolmaster. He speaks of *his* Indians, of *his* forest – he goes deep into it through untrodden ways – and of his streams, along which he travels in search of the unconverted with more zeal than treasure hunters in search of gold.

His life is lived in the utmost poverty yet he has his reward. When he rings the mission bell for Mass each Sunday at six o'clock the families come from far, the men with their faces painted, their white shirts hanging out over their trousers; the women in plain garments of blue cloth gathered in at neck and waist and each with an offering of roots or manioc.

I watched him among all these Indians of hybrid race, with their brown or cinnamon coloured faces and their narrow, indifferent eyes. And as I watched, I wondered. What infinite faith he revealed as he preached his sermons in Kitchua, in his litanies, and in his prayers which the natives echoed after him. I wondered at the secret of his joy amid these impassive, mask-like faces, for he knew how slender was his grip upon his congregation. The witch-doctor, like evil itself, is always present among his flock, and the witch-doctor's power is undiminished and deeper-rooted than his own.

As we took our evening walk along the deserted terrace he acknowledged the fact quite simply. He would have liked a supply of quinine, some injections, a little iodine to help in the struggle, but he had nothing but his bare hands and his ideals. He would never be able to prevent sick people from summoning the medicine man at night and yielding their sores to his lips and incantations.

He knew, too, that in the dry season the traders would come with their engaging smiles and their bags of great quantities of trousers and lace-edged petticoats. And after them would come the seekers after gold, and after them an endless sequence of men in search of profit. Yet I could not say: "Why do you keep up the struggle, Father? Is it for the sake of commerce that you are trying to turn your Indians into gentle, peace-loving men ?" The night was too lovely, too still, broken only by the familiar sound of the streams, for me to utter any bitter thoughts.

As we walked the padre spoke of France. There was emotion in his voice as he talked of "my beautiful country". We knew that behind the altar of the mission chapel there lay the bones of a young Frenchman, Robert Cartigny, who had died mysteriously on a river bank a week's canoe journey away. His body had been brought back to the mission;

only his bones remained to bear witness to his adventurous spirit. There Father Leon watched over them and thus, in a forest unknown to the world, the remains of a dead man kept alive in an old missionary's heart his love for his country.

VII

In the political lieutenant's hut, amid the faded prints and old patriotic calendars which festooned the walls, we organized our journey down the Bobonaza River. We needed seven canoes and 21 *bogas* (the native name in this region for canoeists). The price we had to pay, after bargaining with the native chiefs, the *curaca* with his inevitable gold-ringed staff, the captain and his assistants the *alcedes*, was one *vara* (about a yard) of cloth per man per day – the colour to be left to each man's own choice.

These details settled to everybody's satisfaction, the women immediately began the job of chewing their husband's *masato* while we checked the cases and the canoes, some of which were worm-eaten and let in water. Father Leon, who had been watching all the excitement, led us into the room which served him as study and bedroom and opened a register. The careful details it contained were revealing and disturbing. All the baptized Indians living along the banks of the Bobonaza were listed in a long column. Many of them were dead and in another column the manner of their end was marked with a cross and a date. Some had died of fever, some of *pian* (a form of syphilis), others by malaria. Some had been murdered by the Jivaros or by the Muratos; others had been lost in the forest.

With a sad smile the padre closed his book and presented us with a list of medicinal plants to be found in the region, together with details of their therapeutic use. Some of them had suggestive names: blood leaf, boar's eye (good against haemorrhages), fiery wood.

For the rest we must trust in God...

At dawn, in the mist, we loaded the canoes. The narrow, over-weighted craft sank down till the water reached their rims. We gave last words of warning to the oarsmen, cut the lianas that tethered us to the banks, and at once the powerful current swept the canoes, helpless as dead trees, towards the first rapids of the Bobonaza and the forest of the Amazon.

FOUR : INTO THE FOREST

I

To try to describe the Amazonian forest in terms of figures conveys nothing. You may say that a line drawn from the foothills of the Cordillera of the Andes – a range of mighty granite hills which gradually decline towards the east – drawn right across to the Atlantic would pass through more than 2,500 miles of forest. Draw it diagonally towards the north-east and the figure is nearly 3,200 miles; draw it diagonally to the south-east and the distance rises again, this time to more than 4,400 miles. But you will not comprehend the reason why the Amazon is still largely unknown and probably forever unknowable until you have struggled for many hours to penetrate a few yards of liana-covered marshland. You have only to camp on the bank of one of its rivers to feel yourself in a different world. The explorer must creep into it like a reptile, with a reptile's skill and prudence. The ornithologist, the geographer, the geologist, the anthropologist may venture there, but however much they play the reptile they will scarcely see the forest of the Amazon as it really is.

And when all the tribes that live in the forest have been discovered, all their dialects and languages collected, studied and classified; when all the species and sub-species and groups of birds and mammals have their stuffed representatives proudly exhibited in museums throughout the world; and when the Americans have located and exhausted the oil-wells of the entire continent, when the radio broadcasts its advertisements into the most wretched of the bamboo huts hidden at the tip of some lagoon, even then I doubt whether anyone will have seen the Amazonian forest as it really is. It will have been exploited, that is all.

This is what the forest looked like to our astonished eyes: trees, a limitless expanse of trees reaching upwards to an average height of more than 60 yards; trees packed close to one another and bound together, living and dead, by innumerable creepers; trees that let in only a minimum of light. And, over all, an odour of decay exuding from the soil and forever imprisoned under the thick dome of the foliage. Each single tree is the realm of a multitude of insects, serpents, birds and flowers. Alongside each realm there stands another, with its own customs, rules and dramas. Besides that stands yet another, and then another in countless array... one imagines that perhaps by following them it must be possible to reach one's goal. So have thought the nomadic tribes who for a thousand years have wandered in that world and who will go on wandering there until they have vanished.

The river which took us into this green cavern of stinking life and odorous corruption was swift, powerful and treacherous. The most skilful canoeist finds it difficult to manoeuvre in its current. Stones he on a level with the surface. The river narrows unexpectedly, its depth changes without warning. But our canoeists had good judgment. It was a revelation to watch the art with which they plied their paddles to dodge obstacles and keep their craft head-on down the river whenever it threatened to shift broadside on and sweep helplessly down the current. Only once did their skill fail. On the second day our own canoe was moved too swiftly into midstream, was caught up in the rapids and struck a rock. It began to ship water dangerously and as our oarsmen tried to bring it to the bank the eddies flooded us.

Matter, Guébriant and I, swimming with all our strength against the current, succeeded in bringing to shore the waterproof bags that held the most precious part of our load. But some of the equipment was done for; the sound recorder was damaged, one Exakta camera was unusable and a part of the film, the compass and one altimeter had disappeared. The Indians could not understand our impotent rage, but after this, whenever the stream grew dangerous, we sent them ahead, willy-nilly, to trace out the path for us.

So the days went by. During the long hours of sailing, Guébriant filled his notebooks with figures, Matter studied the light and took some photographs and I looked forward impatiently to one day reaching the tribe we had come to seek. The landscape was monotonous: muddy banks, huge trees, their grandeur hidden by countless parasitic climbing plants, bound by trailing lianas to the squat plants below, which were intensely green and laden with moisture. Only the Chonkamayo tree rose high above the rest, spreading its branches like an ochre-coloured parasol. In the mornings we saw beautiful white *garsas* flying through the mist; at dusk there were the yellow and black *mangoes*. In between we endured the sun and rain on our naked bodies and the sentimental warbling of worthy Ramon Olalla, singing out of tune.

In the evenings we camped out in empty huts on the muddy banks. Each night, when the beds and mosquito nets had been set up, we sat around a smoky fire trying to dry our clothes and eating our feast of sardines, manioc and preserves washed down with a little water stained pink with permanganate. The Indians came, shivering, to lie down near us on wide plantain leaves. Then we would rub oil of camphor on our hands and faces and talc powder on our feet. And so to bed.

Each day of sailing brought us nearer the danger zone. Each day we heard more frequently from the natives of the Upper Bobonaza river the phrase "the heathen". Each day our canoeists became more nervous. Each day we found new islands containing graves. Sometimes the victim had been a Jivaro who had died, far from his tribe, marooned on the island because the natives on the banks were too frightened to let him land. Or sometimes the graves were those of peaceful Indians trapped on the sandy islands when their canoes had been lost while they were sailing in search of salt.

At Sarayacu, a *pueblo* of three huts on the fringe of the Jivaro country, the nervousness of our canoeists at last overwhelmed them and they deserted. The political lieutenant – the last we were to meet – a man completely destitute who went into ecstasies at the sight of our canned food, could be of no help to us in our search for substitutes. His three Mausers – the weapons of his authority – hung in his miserable hut half eaten away with rust. No junk shop would have accepted them. The man himself was crushed and stifled by the forest. He dared not even go out hunting.

But the news of our arrival spread quickly through the forest grapevine. The natives, timid creatures plastered with protective magical paintings, crept up to investigate us and we were delighted to discover that there were plenty of canoes near our camp.

We showed the Indians our cloth and let them look ecstatically into our mirrors. They fingered our material, told us their names, and allowed us to do some doctoring. Many of them had on their bodies the horrible open sores of the syphilitic *pian*.

Guébriant and I gave them injections and were rewarded with eggs, chickens and grateful looks from these poor wretches: old men who sighed as they watched the needle and gentle girls, already hopelessly infected. Thanks to this simple humanitarianism we were able to enlist 22 canoeists and three men who were to remain with us throughout the expedition. The political lieutenant drew up a contract for us without a smile and read it to the natives, who understood nothing except that they would get cloth, quite a lot of cloth.

The canoes were loaded. On the bank an Italian gold-digger gazed at us with melancholy eyes. He, too, was about to cross the forest as far as the Santiago river. After 40 days' exhausting march he was able to reach the spot he sought. I did not know as I watched his figure dwindling out of sight on the bank that in six months' time I would reach the spot where the Jivaros had attacked and murdered him ....

FIVE : THE FIRST JIVARO

I

The days passed. Swiftly we swept down the Bobonaza river towards the Pastaza. We passed Mango Urco, the village where Father Leon's friend Robert Cartigny had met his death six years ago. The Indians who are hostile to the white man say that he was murdered by his companion, another Frenchman. Here we met families of seals playing and grunting around the canoes until Jean warned them off with a crack from his revolver and upset our Indians. To them the death of a lobo means the death of a child within a year. They are less concerned at the fate of the *buffeo*, or sea calf, because according to their legend its death merely provokes women to adultery.

We camped at Mango Urco for the night with palms and bamboos for beds and mosquito nets. During the evening we played the gramophone, much to the satisfaction of our oarsmen. The voice of Minon Vallin set them clasping one another's hands with emotion; operatic music scared them into silence; American jazz provoked universal merriment.

During the brief twilight our camp fires sent out a flickering summons to the hordes of insects and vampires. When we grew tired of rubbing our necks with citronella and squashing great mosquitoes on our foreheads, we climbed inside our protective white tents. Next morning we set out on the three-day journey to the Pastaza river.

II

The Rio Pastaza drains the basin of Ambato, 125 miles from the Pacific, and its black waters run down into the Amazon. We entered it on a July morning, flowing swift and wide. The bank of the river opposite the mouth of the Bobonaza, which bounded our horizon, consisted of one vast wall of sky. At last it was possible for our six canoes to paddle abreast and our oarsmen shot us downstream in high spirits.

Our first objective had been a *pueblo* called Andoas which the geographers, in some doubt about its precise location, have placed much too far south. Actually the real settlement of Andoan Indians was once situated at the junction of the Bobonaza and Pastaza rivers. Today it no longer exists. It was destroyed by the Achual tribe of Jivaro Indians more than 20 years ago.

It was sunset before the rapid current brought our canoes in sight of a dozen huts scattered along the riverside: the only collection of homes along the entire length of the Pastaza, nearly 450 miles. It is called Chambira and it is the place most exposed to raids from the heathens, as Father Leon, that heroic man, who had visited it two years previously, had warned us.

In Chambira dwell a few families of strangely varied character and speech which excited my ethnographical interest. The chief, worn out by fever but still dignified, spoke a dialect new to me called *Chimikae*, but when we came to examine it we found to our delight and astonishment that it is identical with the dialect of Zapparo which is spoken by tribes living much further north in a region quite unlike the Pastaza country. The chief's sons, all skilful fishermen and good navigators, could also speak Kitchua.

We went into the huts, of which the newest were narrow and, contrary to tradition, hastily built. There we collected, one by one, a number of men who seemed to have been brought together by chance. Some were big, with long bodies and straight smooth hair hanging down to their shoulders; others were small with short curly hair. But all of them sat shyly apart from us on their bamboo beds while the scared women hurriedly hid their children in the long grass nearby. "Amigo, amigo," we said, over and over again, trying to tempt them to speech and friendliness with mirrors and red cotton thread. But not until night fell and the festivities in honour of our 20 oarsmen from the Bobonaza were under way, did they lose their fear of us.

III

To me – to us all – these moments at Chambira were fraught with an exciting anticipation. Our camp was pitched on a height, opposite the overturned canoes of the river bank. Around and below us, beyond the fields of manioc and plantain, stretched the vast mysterious territory of the Jivaro Indians. We had reached our first major goal; now it was merely a question of luck and determination before we met the tribesmen themselves. Meanwhile there were the coming festivities to be enjoyed and examined.

Night fell on the remote *pueblo*, hiding the vast forest. In the chief's hut the women stirred up the fires that smoulder traditionally at the heart of three huge logs in front of each bed. Cotton wicks impregnated with wax were lighted. A drum sounded its rapid monotonous beat. The feast of *Chicha* was beginning.

The Indians came in from afar off, making their way with dignity through lianas and giant ferns. They strode on to the mound standing before the chief's hut, the wives first, each husband following her. In token of peace the hut was wide open. From every side the people crowded in and sat down on low bamboo platforms. Guébriant, Matter and I sat in the shadow waiting.

The gravity broke into gaiety when the *chicha* was served. The mass of masticated manoic was held in open jars into which the women plunged their hands before taking the earthenware vessels to each guest. Before each man they halted, continuously stirring the mixture of manioc and water while the men spat on the ground and began to drink.

A young Indian, already tipsy, clung to me, took my pipe from between my teeth and began to swallow the smoke with delight. The crowd burst into laughter and uproariously demanded dances.

Four men and a woman took the centre of the stage for the first dance. The men, beating their drums rhythmically began to move slowly around in a circle. The woman, young and amazingly graceful, stood in the centre and began to dance. Her drapery barely covered her small, firm breasts, and the rapid motion of her legs and the intricate patterns her feet traced on the ground conveyed a strangely sensual excitement. It was the nuptial dance.

Her husband joined her, a splendid creature with painted face and brow decked with red and black feathers. He stood opposite her, stamping fiercely on the ground in time with the beating drums. The girl hung her head and half closed her eyes like some victim in ecstasy. Mutual desire possessed them. The man's impatience, the woman's feverish willingness, traced magic ciphers on the ground while the hushed, motionless spectators sat and watched...

The dance was never finished. As man and woman whirled and stamped and the drumbeats began to rise to a crescendo, an Indian appeared in the light of the fires. The dance stopped immediately. The drunken Indians grew at once uneasy and restrained.

The Indian, naked to the waist and wearing a black and white loincloth, drew near to the chief, spear in hand, and took his place among the drinkers. His name was Aragunasa, the first heathen we had met, the first of the men we had travelled so many thousand miles to see: a Jivaro from the Achual tribe. And these brave Indians of Chambira, dwellers in forest and by rivers, faithful to their huntsman's traditions, could not conceal their dread of him.

IV

Next morning we began our task of persuading Aragunasa to lead us to his tribe. We gathered around him, we three Frenchmen sitting on boxes, Ramon Olalla squatting on his haunches and the old chief standing with his gold-ringed staff of office in his hand. I put the questions in Spanish, Ramon translated them into Kitchua and the chief relayed them to Aragunasa in a language we could not follow, a mixture of Jivaro and Chimikae. The replies came back by the same route in reverse.

"We are your friends. We want to visit your tribe."

"I do not understand."

"Where do your people live? Will you take us there?"

"I do not understand."

"Would you like a piece of cloth?"

"I do not understand."

It took two days of palavering, interspersed with drinking, before Aragunasa consented to take us to his tribe.

Our departure was fixed for next morning at dawn. We rose at five and hurried to load the canoes, glad that the decisive day had come. The river had risen during the night and now covered the shores of the islet. Huge tree trunks floated past but they did not worry our oarsmen; we should travel fast.

At six everything was ready. We waited. Aragunasa did not appear; only the chief came, stepping carefully down the steep bank.

"The Jivaro will not come," he said. "He went off hunting during the night."

Disappointed, we had a hasty pow-wow. We had to make up our minds quickly for our oarsmen, looking worried at the news, and chattering nervously, were gathering around one of their tribe, a native called Santo who had been wounded by a spear during an expedition to the salt districts. We made up our minds. Aragunasa's desertion meant that our only chance of meeting with the Jivaro Indians was to explore every tributary on the right bank of the Pastaza until we found them. It was not an inviting prospect, but if that was the only way they could be found, that was the only way we could go. We gave the word to set off.

Towards midday, under a sky heavy with threatening storms, we reached the first tributary, a river whose dark waters flowed deep into the bed of the Pastaza. By a skilful manoeuvre our six craft veered round to face against the current and the exhausting journey upstream began. Every man strained unceasingly at the paddles for the slightest weakening meant a loss of two or three yards and, worse, a discouragement which could be fatal. In such a struggle morale must be preserved at all costs. Above us a mass of vegetation, heavy with mud and corruption, pressed the trees down over our heads. Some of the trees had broken under the weight and their rotting carcasses, floating downstream, made our task more difficult still.

It was evening before the river suddenly widened into a regular lagoon and the merciless current dwindled until it was placid as a lake. Aquatic plants and palm trees transformed the lagoon into a mysterious garden – but a garden fraught with danger, for the problem now was how to gain solid ground. As far as we Europeans could see, there was no landing place along the shores of the lagoon because the heavy foliage pressed right down to the water's edge in a forbidding wall. We need not have worried. We had not reckoned with our Indian's instinctive skill and before nightfall they had discovered a narrow channel leading to an island.

As we sighted it my heart leapt. For a moment I thought that we had come to journey's end for there, clear and unmistakable on the shore, was a pathway and, at the end of the pathway, a hut whose elliptical roof, the way the fires were disposed, and the pottery vessels lying scattered around betrayed the hut of a Jivaro.

We landed and made our way up the path. My heart fell. Inside there were no traces of any occupants. The fires were cold, the pottery abandoned. Perhaps if we dug beneath the beds we might find skeletons, but, valuable though they would have been for our researches, this was scarcely the moment to scare our men who were growing increasingly fearful. They lit fires and made soup and the night passed without alarms other than the customary visits of the vampires and mosquitoes.

Our log book for the next few days tells of similar researches and anxieties. We hunted right and left in the forest and found nothing definite, only suggestive traces: bamboo fences set up for fishing, mangroves with signs, even the framework of a canoe rotted with river mud. We searched. We called. But we startled only the pairs of big blue and yellow *aras* in the topmost branches of the trees and the bands of howling monkeys.

V

We went back once, and then a second time, to the river Pastaza. Fortunately its violent current carried the canoes southward and quietened the protests of our oarsmen who betrayed their discontent by the strokes of their paddles and, at night, by their long whispered discussions at the fireside.

On a lagoon which our Indians called Huagramona we found a Jivaro camp where the hearth was still warm. Carefully we moored our six boats; the luggage was covered with palm leaves and each of us set about his evening tasks. Our menu consisted of grilled parrot, boiled manioc and tea.

We sat red-eyed in the thick of the smoke to avoid the infernal onslaught of the anopheles, eating hurriedly, when our dog Martin, keeping watch, disturbed us all with his raucous barks directed towards a corner of the shadows. Ramon pulled an old revolver from his case and looked at us. Santo, trembling with fear, drew near me and, grasping my arm, cried: "The heathen! The heathen!"

Our 20 men had no more than four of five spears with them to protect them against unpleasant surprises; they lacked even the strength to run and get the canoes. They remained standing, offering a motionless target against the light of the camp fire. But nothing living emerged from outside our circle.

Fred, his pistol in his right hand, his electric torch in his left, advanced towards the trees, followed only by the dog. A slight stir in the leaves just ahead of the beam of light showed that something or someone had fled. The dog was quietened, the alarm subsided. I returned to the fire where Jean, imperturbable and hungry, was still munching his portion of parrot.

That night our oarsmen held a long conference around the fire. When the fierce

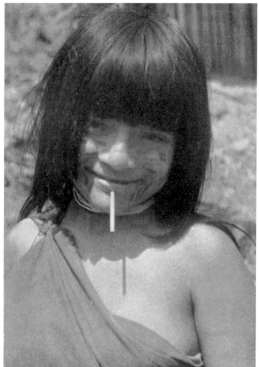

battering of the rain against the roof of our hut abated a little, we overheard the terrified creatures' excited flow of talk. Next day we were not surprised when, after the midday halt on an island in the Pastaza, the oldest informed us of their common decision: they would go no further. They had reached the limit of their endurance and must go home.

Without waiting to hear our opinion, the old fellow went back to his comrades and they set to work unloading our cases. We had to nag at them before they would condescend to put up a shelter for us. Their impatience rose to frenzy when the sun went down and we had difficulty in persuading our three Indians, Isidro, Juan and Santo, whom we had engaged for the duration of the expedition, to stay with us. But at last our arguments won the day; they remained faithful to us and kept their canoe, despite the ironical invitations of the other oarsmen.

When the whole of our load was deposited under the protective roof of plaited palm-leaves, and our beds set up under a provisional *rancho*, the Indians left us without a word. They had forgotten our wandering life together, the dangers shared. The forest annuls everything but the fear of the moment.

They pushed feverishly at the long poles that helped them upstream. Darkness fell. One red gleam glowed back to us from the river; the torch that one of the *bogas* carried to light their night's fire. Gradually it dwindled and disappeared.

We were alone on an island little more than half a mile long, narrow and crested with palm trees. On one side ran the deep, turbulent river; on the other the island was subject to flooding. It was difficult to imagine a more utterly lonely spot in the heart of an unknown region.

We had three men in charge of a load intended for 50; a taxidermist who was, no doubt, highly skilled at preparing his birds but who had misled us as to his knowledge of Indian dialects; only one canoe, and, finally, our three selves, our resolution still undaunted despite the climate, the insect-bites and our perilous position.

Next day, at dawn, we walked round the island. From its southern tip we could clearly see the mouth of a river, the Rio Siguin, so Santo informed us. Isidro called it by another name, far more complicated, so we chose Siguin. This river would give us our last chance of finding the Achual Jivaros. If we failed, the success of our expedition would be jeopardized and our own lives would be in danger.

There was too little room in the canoe for us all, so I chose Ramon and the *bogas* Isidro and Santo to accompany me. Juan was to stay with Matter and Guébriant in charge of our belongings. My freight consisted of a bed and mosquito nets, first-aid kit, a few objects for bargaining, my hunting rifle and my faithful Colt at my belt.

We parted on the shore, with the utmost calm. As the canoe swept into the Siguin river I turned back and waved. On the bank of the island my friends waved back, cheerful despite their complete isolation. Their lives now depended on me, for without a canoe they were marooned in the middle of the river. If for any reason I failed to return their lives would be forfeit.

VI

Towards midday, tired of paddling, we landed. The forest, fairly thin at this point, promised easy walking; but at the first step the ground gave way and Ramon sank in stinking mud up to his waist. We pulled him out and dipped him in the river, and the gods, no doubt appeased by this last sacrifice, showed themselves favourable to our quest. Near the tip of a huge lagoon, dotted with palm-leaves, I noticed a hut perched high up on an island. The canoe glided through the aquatic undergrowth and ran ashore near a path. I darted forward eagerly but the hut was empty, given over to termites, ants and giant spiders. But my disappointment was short-lived, for Santo, who was watching the impressive landscape of forest and water that gleamed before us in the sunshine, uttered a cry:

"*Canu... canu...* A boat!"

It was too far off for the oarsmen to be distinguished, but it was travelling fast. We made a note of its direction and, full of hope, launched out again on the lagoon.

An hour later our quest had ended. We were at last among the Jivaros.

SIX : CHARMING "THE HEATHEN"

I

We steered our canoe against the bank near a hut which consisted of a roof of plaited palm leaves hanging down to within two yards of the ground on a foundation of posts set out in oval shape. No sound, no smoke betrayed the presence of living creatures; and yet there they were: eight Jivaros, standing beside their bamboo beds, waiting, watching me attentively. In the middle, seated with dignity on a stool, a half-naked Indian, whom I took to be the chief, was quietly smoothing his long black hair.

I marched up to him and held out my hand. He took no notice. He did not understand my gesture of goodwill. I made a sign to Ramon, who unpacked a few objects – mirrors, needles and thread. The man cast an indifferent eye over our wares and, still smoothing his hair with one hand, uttered a single word: *"Nuha!"*

At the word an elderly woman, wearing a white loin cloth, shuffled forward from the far end of the hut. It was to her that we must give our presents. In exchange, she brought me a heap of roots and a vessel full of foaming *chicha*. Now was the time to prove my good intentions; I swallowed the thick beverage at one draught.

The brown and painted faces relaxed. First two, then three, Indians drew near, their hands open. Still in silence, I sat down beside the chief; they could have the whole evening to look at me, to touch my shirt, my cap, my boots. The rest was a matter of patience.

When the sun had almost sunk to the level of the lagoon a number of canoes drew up besides ours. Indians came running up the short slope to the hut, the women in front, naked to the waist, bent under the weight of a child or a load of manioc, then the men, glistening with sweat, their bows on their shoulders, their quivers full of darts hanging against their chests. Without glancing at our group they laid down their weapons, hung their poison-cases over their beds and demanded *chicha*.

When they had drunk they came towards us and formed a silent semicircle. They were fine-looking warriors and huntsmen, but their painted faces were hostile. Only one gave me a friendly look. I learned later that he had known white men, trappers, who had given him the name of Baotista. He was the most dangerous of them all.

Night came quickly, without dusk. The women fanned the fires with their breath while the naked children played at battles. All over world there is a certain melancholy about the close of day; we felt it here. The men, stretched on their beds, spoke to one another in grave tones, telling in words I could not follow of the day's hunting, struggles and anxieties. Sometimes a shadow moved between two fires, performing actions which meant nothing to me. I simply sat and watched: I felt no fear, only an immense joy. At last

I had realized the hope formed so long ago, and reached the goal sought for so many days!

How can I explain this unfamiliar emotion? The discovery had been as gradual as the slow progress of the canoe up the river. As the forest grew thicker and more impenetrable, overloaded with its own richness, the Indians had become wilder, wearing loin-cloths instead of trousers and replacing the sign of the Cross by magic paintings. And now those who were lying by my side – were they asleep or spying on me? – were called Jivaros.

Naïvely, I told myself that I would soon find out all about them: the exact colour of their skin, the shape of their skulls, their measurements, the characteristics of their eyes, their ears, their hair. I would learn their language, word by word and in spite of themselves, through the power of signs they would not understand, I would take back to the outside world a picture of these people as they had never been painted before.

It was a great responsibility. I knew some travellers whose immediate reaction would be the contemptuous word "savages". I knew others who would reach for their Bibles and other who, if ever they should wander so far from all the grand hotels of the outside world would, with a blasé air, prepare to bring corruption.

For safety's sake, Ramon and I set up our beds side by side, without a mosquito net. There were few mosquitoes, for that matter, only small vampire bats flitting slyly about.

At dawn the men rose and gathered in the centre of the hut to drink their warm infusion of *awayusa* and tell each other their dreams in whispers. I scarcely awoke.

"You've slept well," Ramon said, surprised, his face pale. He, too, was afraid of the Jivaros.

During the morning we discovered that the younger of Baotista's two wives could speak Kitchua and, through her, we explained our wishes to the chief. There were other white men, we told him, with other cases, more presents! The chief admired my gun. Were there other such things among the other cases? Yes, there were plenty of arms if only he would help us to bring them from the island.

That same day I guided four canoes to my friends and brought them to the camp.

II

The first days of our stay in the Jivaros' hut was a period of waiting. The Jivaros, segregated in their lives and language, were completely unresponsive to our advances. Their hostility had mellowed to indifference. We had to take care not to arouse it again.

Each day's occupations were the same: at dawn the hunters went off into unknown territories, sure-footed and supple. They returned at midday, their bodies gleaming with sweat, and threw down at the foot of their beds the quarry they had shot: big monkeys, toucans or wild pigs.

Two or three men remained beside us, sharpening short darts or drinking sour *yamanche*. Our activities did not interest them.

The children, on the other hand, were as playful as kittens. They enjoyed watching us – it was a new game and they made us join in their dances round the spears stuck in the ground, though as soon as the women saw them they promptly called them away or sent them to fill big calabashes at the river.

We had agreed to beware of the female of the species as of a trap. As they sat at their looms or prepared manioc over their jars, they stared at us unceasingly. They were filthy dirty, with faces adorned only by a small stick thrust through the lower lip, and with pendulous breasts. They certainly awoke no passions in us, but one is apt to behave towards even the least attractive woman with a certain degree of familiarity which the jealous Indians would not have forgiven.

It was essential that the Jivaros should first get used to our presence among them and then to consider it as an advantage to their tribe. Our guns made relations easier. The chief was the first to try them all out in turn – even my heavy Mauser pistol, whose kick gave him an unpleasant surprise – by firing at a tree trunk where the children ripped their fingers digging out shot and bullets. His first shot won our astonished admiration by his skill and the sureness of eye. We established our reputation as marksmen by shooting down a kingfisher in mid-flight! The chief promptly tried to imitate us; but the heavy rifle I gravely offered him hurt his shoulder more than he hurt the innocent humming-birds he aimed at.

This harmless rifle-play won us a certain timid respect, but it was the gramophone which turned the tables in our favour and, to judge by their round eyes and gaping mouths, invested us with magical powers.

When we put on the first record they surrounded us tumultuously. Our closed lips left them in no doubt about the source of the music and the machine was regarded with the awe due to a totem.

"*Takcha! Takcha!*... Again! Again!" they yelled in wild excitement as we turned the handle.

The fire flickered red on their faces; their eyes shone with delight, astonishment, terror. Maceo, the witch-doctor, with his long wavy hair; Kuhi the cunning craftsman and warrior, Vitiap the fisherman; Uriki the traveller; Kantse, whose name means fly, the most agile and skilful archer of them all – these men of the forest, lost in the forest and absorbed by it as the saint dreams of being absorbed by God, all gathered round the gramophone saying, "*Takcha! Takcha!*" insatiably and untiringly as, hour after hour, the black discs turned for them regardless of labels.

That formed the first link between us, but we had other ways of bringing about a speedy friendship: lighters, electric torches, canned food. We gave presents liberally and they took them eagerly. We did not care; the time was coming when they would have to give us something in return.

III

Ten days spent investigating the hut and reconnoitring about the lagoon convinced us that we had found a fruitful region for our work. Already visitors were arriving from the nearby Jivaro villages to inspect the white men, with feathered heads and travelling staffs in hand. There was a mass of information to be gathered, a host of pictures to be taken. But first we had to build a hut as close as possible to our friends. We explained this to the chief by means of the few words we had learned, together with *tarachi*, which means cloth. He led us in his canoe as far as the large island opposite his dwelling. There, amid trees and branching ferns, he spread out both powerful arms.

"*Hea!* The house," he said. Then he counted on his fingers and, with a gesture, suggested the course of the sun. "*Chikitchik Kinda... chikitchik...* a day." He repeated the word five times.

And five days later the site lay exposed to the sun. The hill-side had been cleared of trees by machetes and fire. Enormous bonfires flamed on every side, fed constantly by the women with branches and creepers. Before setting up the supporting posts we took measurements: 25¼ feet by 32 feet 9 inches with the floor raised four feet from the ground and a roof of plaited palm-leaves in the Jivaro tradition. I used a liana three feet long as a yardstick.

The Indians threw themselves into the work with our tools as though it were some wonderful game which, accustomed as they were to living on floors of beaten earth, they could not understand. At midday the women brought them boiled manioc and small fishes that the children had caught wrapped in plantain leaves. The men grew wildly excited about the work; they gave up hunting for the sake of it, and put up with a meagre diet in the evening when they returned.

Their activity was a revelation. I was used to the men of the Andes, unemotional, inert, depressed slaves first of the soil and then of their masters; and the sight of these enthusiastic Indians set me wondering afresh. Had the influence of the Cordillera, of alien oceans and civilizations, moulded the native American to render him unrecognizable, to make him the enemy of his archetype, whom we now saw before us? Or had these families from a freer land preserved their primitive energy with the tenacity of exiles? Whatever the reason, the fact was undeniable; the first test had proved the Jivaros' independence. They delighted in action, in efficient movements. They laughed with pride when they laid low the finest trees in their forest. They sympathized with the law of destruction and renewal which is nowhere more fully realized than in the Amazonian forest; every hour that brought nearer the erection of the camp on the ruins of charred wood stimulated their impatience and their delight. Like other free men, they enjoyed discipline, exertion and rest. And they showed the free man's modesty; no sooner was the last piece of bamboo floor laid down than they made for their huts once more, standing upright in the canoes while the women paddled them.

PART TWO : FINDING

ONE : THERE ARE NO SAVAGES

I

Now that the Jivaros were our friends, at least for the time being, and our hut was built, we settled down to our self-appointed tasks of investigating the habits, lives, customs and physical data of these remote Indians. During the ensuing weeks and months our lives were spent watching them loving and living, hunting and fishing, in courage and in fear, at home and on the march. Thus our story becomes not a voyage across continents, but an exploration into the minds of men and women; and, if confusion is to be avoided, it is now necessary to abandon for a while the chronological order of story-telling in favour of a series of pen-portraits: of the tribe as a whole, of the individuals in it, and of their occupations.

II

The only organized force and the only authoritative voice which the Jivaro Indian obeys is the power of the witch-doctor. The forest dwellers' individualism nullifies any sort of social organization and, in the last resort, any unified system of defence. The 6,000 to 8,000 Indians who make up the Jivaro society live scattered over a vast territory and are united only by bonds of custom, technique and language. There is no authority with power to impose war, to order expeditions, to render justice. The chief, or more correctly the headman, has a part to play in religious or magical ceremonies (as we were to see during the head-shrinking process) but he has only advisory rights. He is listened to only because of his experience and knowledge of customs, as his brother will be listened to after his death. He gives no orders.

The huts, sometimes one or two days' journey apart on foot or by boat, hold groups of eight families, sometimes more. As far as it is possible to make any definite statement about a fact so difficult to ascertain, these communities do not correspond to clans, unless one accepts the notion that a clan consists merely of people living in the same territory and bound to mutual aid and, if necessary, to vengeance for one another's sake.

The basic form of social organization among these Indians appears to be the enlarged family unit. A bond of kinship united all the inhabitants of a single hut. Sons live there with the wives they have brought from outside the hut. If the family increases the children build a dwelling for themselves close to the father's hut, and there is constant communication between them. When a hunting or fishing expedition into neighbouring country is necessary, with the need to set up a temporary camp there, father and son join forces.

In attempting to assess the Jivaros and similar tribes, we tend to look at the Indian way of life from a European point of view, to seek certainty and limitations where independence is the rule, or else, when we see things being done according to some strict rule, to read into them a moral meaning that they do not possess. We find it hard to understand an organization so foreign to our ideas. But one thing is certain: the Jivaros are not savages. There are no such things as savages. All men are civilized. True, they may stand very low on the scale of civilization; but nevertheless they have their place there. A graph of men's position on this scale would be incomplete if it did not include cannibals. Besides, such a division – civilized men on the one hand, savages on the other – is too facile. Where should we draw the line? Since it is easy to identify a population by calling it French or German, we should do the same for these forest-dwelling tribes with their varying degrees of development. We should call them Murato or Jivaro, or, to be precise, Chuor. Each individual knows his name, as he knows the bonds that connect him with his forest, his rivers, his hunting grounds. Here in these remote regions of the Upper Amazon he knows his land and he knows his dead, unquestionably, with greater accuracy than many others do. To defend these possessions, wherein his security lies, the Jivaro is always ready to fight, to kill and to die according to his accepted rules.

What confuses our judgement of the Jivaro and other inhabitants of the virgin forest and makes some of us call them "savages" is that we focus attention on the superficial aspects of their condition. They deserve more serious consideration.

Look, for instance, at Etse, whose name means "The Fly" as he hollows out a canoe. The huge tree he has chosen lies near the river, cut off at shoulder-height. Etse thins down the hulk, striking the wood alternately with his stone axe and the iron axe provided by us. Leaves, lianas, branches are sent flying; insects scatter. The forest rings with a booming sound that echoes afar or stops, mysteriously, before an invisible barrier. It is close and sultry. Etse has kept the feather ornaments in his hair or, rather, he carefully arranged them this morning before leaving his hut, and no less carefully traced the appropriate paintings on his face. Like the righteous man, he fears God or one or other of God's manifestations.

Etse works patiently, making use of the supple lianas that trail around his little glade; he pins them with sharp slips of *chonta* wood to the scarcely hollowed trunk. Thus he ensures the shape of the future canoe before the charring work is begun.

Is Etse skilful? Yes, indeed, and all the others – whose names mean Sun, Dog, River – are like him: skilful in all they undertake. Kuhi the craftsman shows his skill in making his blow-gun, the women in weaving fine loincloths, Maceo the witch-doctor in tending his patients. In all these things Etse is like the workmen the world over; and not only in skill. Look at his body. There is nothing abnormal about it; no ostrich feathers grow at the base of his spine, he has all his teeth and they are well preserved. His measurement card tells us that he is bracycephalic, mesorhynian; adherent lobule, height 5 ft. 3 ins. True, he paints magical signs on his face but there is nothing to prove that they are less effective than other signs. They must be considered highly effective against the attacks of his enemies; and even if they are not, what then? They represent a mystical power as opposed to force, they ennoble the man who traces them on his face. True, also, that he and his kinsmen wear mutilations: those of the ear-lobe for instance. These are usually set down under the heading of adornment; the Jivaro thread bamboo ornaments through the holes that deform their ears, and these long tubes of bamboo in turn carry feathers of brilliant colours. But they are not the only people in the world who thread strange objects through their ears. We tend to wonder and laugh at the costume of these so-called savages. But if we look at coloured prints illustrating the evolution of costume in Europe, we see that not only have style, cut and material undergone countless changes but that all these pictures of the past seem pointless and absurd, mere fancy dress. Our grandfathers, staring smugly over their stiff high collars, are not less peculiar. As far as one can retrace the history of the Jivaro and other tribes, one finds the same black and white loin-cloth, the same festal headdress, down through the generations. Nothing has changed. The father would recognize his son without difficulty.

I look at Etse as he lies daydreaming now, with his arm outstretched towards the palm-leaf roof. I wonder what, next to his costume and the colour of his skin, would most surprise a European suddenly confronted with him.

In my opinion it would be the fact that our Etse has no watch: no watch, no watch-chain, no chain of any sort.

The Jivaro, like all "savages", are free from the tyranny of time. The passing hours and days are noticed only by the needs of nature: they get hungry about midday and again towards six or seven in the evening; they wake at dawn with no other alarm than the insects buzzing among the trees, just as the big aras or small parakeets set off to hunt for seeds when the sun rises and, when night comes, fly in bands towards the islands where they like to sleep.

His physiological reactions govern his individual life. The course of the sun governs his social activity, as fisherman, hunter or warrior. He can distinguish between soon and late, long and short. If I ask Etse: "Is your brother's hut far off?" he stretches out his arms and nods. "*Ae, ae.*" ("Yes. A long way"). Then he sketches the course of the sun:

once round, twice round and a bit more. So it is more than two days' journey away.

Another Jivaro, tougher than Etse, contradicts him. "*Tsa*," he says. "It is a short way." But he gives the sun's course the same length as Etse. It means that to reach the hut it takes two days and a few hours' walking or sailing (the speed is the same). For Etse the journey seems long because he gets tired, for the other it seems short because he does it without fatigue. No doubt this system of measuring time has its limitations – it leaves vague both the past and the future. It is true that the Jivaro sets little store by fixed dates, but if it so happens that they have a definite appointment – in some hunting ground, for instance – they tie knots on a rope to indicate the days. I saw this done once when they had to bring back to our camp a good supply of manioc. When they left there were seven knots on the rope. Seven days later the canoes drew up to land, filled with roots.

For certain remote events we sometimes heard them say the word *embuash* (kapok). "When the kapok flowers..."

Sometimes they even note the movements of the *musachi*, the Little Bear, in the starlit sky.

They can count up to three; but the humble unit, *chikitchik*, is usually enough for them – they merely repeat it as often as necessary.

Such simplicity is not merely superficial. To maintain direct contact with the soil, to harmonize his activities with the incessant metamorphoses of nature and of the beings that surround him, is a prime necessity for the inhabitant of the forest. Why should one, how can one, separate things that are intimately united? Nature is impressive, sometimes terrifying; it is easy to understand how, in addition, it assumes a supernatural significance. Trees, creepers, animals, things that crawl and things that fly all form part, in varying degrees, of a single chain of existence that it would be rash to break.

Etse, from birth to death, remains in contact with his soil. He is extremely conservative and traditionalist, but will accept improvements to his lot and to his technique. He can recognize that a gun is an asset for war-making and an axe for boat-building. Here again the epithet "savage" is out of place. His environment offers him restricted possibilities – sand, wood, a few stones. These are the instruments of progress for him, and he scarcely expects to escape from these limitations or to receive help from outside. He must depend on what he has got: and this poverty is an obstacle to the improvement of his condition.

Fred Matter, during our evening conversations, sometimes told us about the Eskimos, who are certainly more advanced than our Indians, cleverer and more adaptable. But they have a confused conception of progress. If they enjoy its benefits, it is because they have been imposed on them. For races that live in permanent contact with the soil the ideal is not progress but stability. Therein lies security, the certainty that tomorrow will be like today.

TWO : THE HUNTSMEN

I

Kuhi, the craftsman, whose profile resembles that of the Northern Indians, sat on the river bank making a blow-gun. Across two forked stakes he laid a long, slender branch of grey wood, previously polished on the outside. From an earthernware vessel standing by him he took some sand and moistened it with little dabs of water. With his right hand he spread it over the wood and laid across the first branch another, equally long and slender. The process of polishing began: a rapid friction to and fro to produce on both parts of the gun an equally smooth and even surface. Kuhi was absorbed in his task; he did not raise his head as a woman went past to fetch water from the river in her big calabash. His young son Piasé watched him, motionless.

The making of a blow-gun is a fascinating process at which the Indians excel both by the simplicity of their technique and by the perfection of the result. If we spent whole hours and days watching its various stages this is what we should see:

The two branches, having been polished inside, are subjected to the action of a rod of very hard wood to scrape away a hollow tube inside. For this, Kuhi sets up in a straight line three strong stakes 4½ feet in height and about 2½ feet apart, the last of which stands under the eaves of the hut to protect it from rain. Near the tip of each stake he makes a notch; the first piece of wood is laid there, held in place by wedges called *naspak*. The rod of *chonta* palm, over ten feet long, called *tsinsan-makash*, is smeared with damp sand and placed between the two pieces of wood. It projects a little less than a foot on the side nearest the hut. Here the craftsman grasps it, and drives it with a rhythmical to-and-fro movement for two whole days. The apparatus is firmly held together by means of tough and supple lianas, passed under the lugs of the wedges and wound round the work.

With his arms half-stretched and his hands at shoulder-level, Kuhi pulls and pushes at the *tsinsan-makash*. Sometimes he tests the strength of the lianas, sometimes he rubs more damp sand on the rod. After two hours' work he has to check up on the wedges, note any faults and tighten the couplings. What neatness, what infinite care, he brings to his task. Passing his hand over the barrel of the blow-gun, which is being hollowed out smoothly through the regular friction of the fibres, the Indian comments with satisfaction: "*Tupni. Tupnitei...* It is straight."

After four or five days' work we can see the central groove completed, its diameter slighter wider on the side from which the dart is to be ejected. Then he proceeds to fine down the weapon by scraping away the external surface with an instrument something like a plane with a triangular handle. This is the *tsingen*, easy to handle and capable of removing fine shavings.

About nine inches from the tip, a mouthpiece is cut with a knife. Here the bone mouthpiece will ultimately be inserted. The two sections are then glued together with resin. Sticking the inside takes barely a quarter of an hour. The gummed surfaces are held to the fire while the joint is bound with a thin, tough liana. When it has set, the outside is given a final polishing and the weapon is handed over to an Indian who specializes in finicky jobs. His task is to remove the first binding of liana and replace it with a careful binding of an even slenderer liana. Varnish is then spread over it to conceal any unevenness, it is smoothed by heat and polished with manioc bark and the completed weapon has an effect of gleaming newness which wins the admiration of all the group.

II

One day, soon after we had settled in our new hut, the chief came to wake us at dawn. I drew aside my mosquito-net and saw him standing in the mist, equipped for hunting with his long blow-gun over his shoulder and his quiver slung round his neck and hanging across his chest. He proposed to take us for a long hunting-trip in the region of the Upper Siguin, near a hut where his elder son Vitiap, the fisherman, lived. We left Ramon and two bogas to guard the camp, while we three Europeans and Isidro went down to the canoes.

We sailed for a long time along the lagoon, amid the noisy flutter of all the water-birds hunting for food. In the tops of the palm-trees small yellow and green parrots watched us from between the leaves. The great *aras* fled at our approach; we heard their hoarse cries echoing in the distance. We saw brown *sin-sin*, which fly as clumsily as a domestic hen, but whose flesh is uneatable. We shot at them to stop their infuriating cries. A single volley from ten yards away, to the delight of the Indians, sent a whole branchful of them into the water. The explosions scared a cloud of humming-birds and sent them soaring into the sky.

Each time we sailed on it the lagoon revealed fresh beauties. The canoe led us through an ever-changing labyrinth. Paddling was easy work on this smooth lake where the only obstacles were roots at the surface of the water. And the sky above it was patterned with palm-leaves and tall upright trunks that were an unceasing delight to the eye.

Suddenly the canoe ahead increased its speed and drew near a small island of mud covered with brushwood. The chief, half erect, held in his right hand a short spear with a sharp tip of *chonta* wood. As he moved, the craft grounded. The spear was flourished high in the air for a moment and then darted towards the ground. There was an eddy; as we drew up we saw a fine cayman dashing off through the muddy water. We were awkwardly placed for shooting at it, and in any case it was too late; the reptile had disappeared. The chief, without a sign of disappointment, picked up his floating spear again and gave his children the word to resume their paddles.

A little later we reached the mainland and went ashore where a path led through a narrow glade. The forest was dark, although the sun was already high. Mosquitoes surrounded us immediately and drove us onward. The hunt had begun.

We walked in single file. The two boys and their father picked up their long loin-cloths and tucked them under their belts of liana. We went on, seeing nothing but the back of the man in front, hearing nothing but the rustle of eaves or branching ferns as we pushed them aside. We advanced slowly. Long minutes passed, then more long minutes. Even amid this unvaryingly green nature, whose pattern recurred to infinity, we still retained a sense of time; it was as though our weariness were linked to a clock-face. We caught ourselves counting seconds as if, the sixtieth or the hundredth, something wonderful was going to happen, and then starting on a fresh hundred which we counted with intensified anxiety.

On desert tracks the explorer becomes obsessed and finally maddened by the monotonous rhythm of his own step; in the forest, it is the passing of seconds that drives one mad.

The Indians kept on walking, parting the lianas with quiet movement of their bent arms. We could not tell what track they were following: monkey, peccary or *coati*. We crossed marshes whose stench was stifling. Treading barefoot through this mud, as they had trodden on prickly roots, the hunters never hurried; their only concern now was to avoid being bitten by the snakes which abound in these parts. But the only snake we saw, frightened at our approach, glided through the leaves and disappeared.

At midday we stopped near a stagnant pool to prepare and drink our strengthening *yamanche*. We completed the meal with a tablet of Ovomaltine and the tip of a palmetto which Matter cut down with his knife. During this halt we suffered a savage attack from mosquitoes. The Indians bore it stoically, crushing the insects with great slaps. Red marks multiplied on their brown skins, but they did not utter a word.

The meal ended we set off again. The forest has been described as a wall; it is a nightmare wall, which one can get into but never through. Every two seconds you take a step, you part the creepers, breaking them with a sharp snap, the wall disappears and then reappears before and behind you. But at last this prisoners' march through the darkness came to an end.

The hunter held out his arm, pointing. Suddenly, as though towards a glimpse of light, we all rushed forward. Where was the quarry? The Indian raised his blow-gun through the leaves, inserted into the barrel his poisoned dart feathered with cotton fluff, puffed out his cheeks and the first projectile flew off.

The quarry was a big *coati*, something like a badger but larger and longer-bodied. It leapt about from branch to branch, stopped a minute and leapt off again. The hunter glided swiftly through the lianas, keeping parallel to his quarry as though he meant to

deceive it by apparent indifference. We lost them both from sight; only the brushwood stirring as they passed through it showed where they had gone. In the middle of a glade we caught sight of the animal perched on a tree-trunk, picked out by a sunbeam against the dark green and forming a splendid target. The hunter, a few steps from us, held his blow-gun aloft with both hands and fired again.

The *coati* was hit. We saw it struggle, shake its long head and dart into the undergrowth. The children rushed after it. As we tried to follow, the hunter stopped us.

"*Tsa tsa*. No," he said. "Wait."

Two minutes later the animal was before us, stiff, without a single bloodstain on its dark fur. Tsamarin, the chief's son, beaming with joy, held it dangling from his outstretched hand.

We set off once more, not knowing in what direction. Neither Jean nor Fred nor I could tell whether we were going back to the lagoon or towards Vitiap's hut.

As dusk fell I shot at and wounded a shrill-voiced bird of prey; four or five of the same species hovered round the spot where it fell, making even louder cries. The time had come to shoot. We shared the job between the three of us and for a few minutes shots rang out noisily in the forest. Tsamarin ran gaily to pick up the birds, tying their feet together with a liana. But his father never smiled; he was a man who disliked noise.

III

That night Fred Matter, who was aching to film a hunt, described his plan to us. He had not been able to take his camera with him on this expedition, because to get good results he would have to stay near the camp and choose a part of the forest where it was not too dark. His experience among the Eskimos was not valid for the Jivaro country, with its different conditions of climate and light. Moreover the natives of Angmassali had not been afraid of the camera, while here the simplest unexpected gesture awoke mistrust. But Fred had his plan to take the pictures. His only worry was the dampness of the forest. In his dark-room, constructed of plaited palms and broad leaves, he had succeeded in developing only bits of grey film. Perhaps a developing-bath, or some warm water, would solve the problem; we hoped so. Meanwhile, Matter plunged with enthusiasm into a fat volume of detective stories. Under his mosquito-net his light shone white, late into the night.

IV

A few days later Fred put his plan into action. The sun shone brightly, the lagoon had fallen during the last two days, revealing a muddy bottom and families of caymans asleep in the shallow water. We were going on another hunting expedition.

Two Indians were waiting for us at the bottom of our ladder. They carried their blow-guns over their shoulders, but today we had left our guns behind and were to be merely spectators.

We made our way into the forest quite near our island. The ground was fairly dry, which made walking easier; from time to time a sunbeam shone on a tall fern, making it glow like a stained-glass window.

At the first halt to sharpen the darts, Fred tried to explain what he wanted. Seizing a hunter's weapon, he pretended to insert a dart, to aim and blow. After a moment's hesitation, the Indian laughed and imitated him. "*Make, make!* Perfect!" cried Fred, and out came his camera from its case and up to his eye. "*Takcha*. Do it again," he commanded.

Then the lens, at its maximum aperture, followed the course and the gestures of the Indians. The mimicry proved as enthralling as the actual hunt. The two men, no longer concerned with killing, threw themselves into the game without restraint. They mimed the stalking of their prey, the preparation of the darts which they drew from their quivers and rolled in the left hand before shooting them recklessly into the heart of the untenanted undergrowth. All the darts were poisoned!

By an amazing piece of luck, a big monkey sat motionless on a branch, a black shape against the shimmering background of leaves. The hunter nearest him lowered his weapon, already raised in play. His face grave, he seemed to be waiting for some secret message before creeping towards the animal, which bounded forward. Surprised by the unexpected turn of events, we tried to follow him.

Our procession of spectators and beaters broke through the brushwood as far as the edge of the manioc plantation. Matter, as he came out into the sunlight, saw the monkey hanging from a high branch. It had been hit. Fred quickly raised his camera and managed to film the animal's dying spasms and its vain efforts to get rid of the dart that pierced its flank before it fell dead at our feet.

Immediately the Indians tossed their weapons into the air and burst into a fit of laughter so prolonged and so intense that it was almost painful to hear.

V

Big game is rare in the forests of the Upper Amazon. Pumas, black jaguars and tapirs do not tempt the Indian hunter. Their flesh is not food, and no religious tradition has marked them down as victims. Their rarity would in itself be enough to preserve them from the spears and poisoned arrows of the *Chuor* – the name the Jivaros give themselves – who do not care for stalking or for lengthy pursuits. Only the monotonous cry of the wild dog can rouse these Indians from their indifference; to capture this creature they organize beats which, however, rarely meet with success.

What quarry is he after, then, this man who goes off before dawn armed with only a wooden spear? We learn the answer from the sets of jaws which he sticks into the palm thatch above the terrace of his hut: peccary. These mammals of the hog family are plentiful in the region bounded by the rivers Pastaza and Morona. Travellers who have met them in other parts of Northern America have described their habits, their customs, the ferocity with which they defend themselves when attacked. The Indian is perfectly aware of the danger; yet he always sets off alone on their trail. He walks slowly, in absolute silence. The sharp point of his spear precedes him through brushwood and tangled creepers. Even the monkeys do not scamper away as he passes, as though some instinct tells them that the hunter is after some other prey.

By what signs the hunter guides himself to the peccary we were never able to discover. It is easy to establish the habits of pumas and small tigers by means of their tracks, and to wait for them where you choose, but peccaries live in herds and are constantly on the move. They leave a path four or five yards wide where they have broken through the forest; but this is an inconclusive clue, for they return to the same path only if the whole herd, in the grip of some collective panic, is driven backwards. Thus the hunter will not follow the trail that the peccaries have made but try to anticipate and find the exact spot where the hurrying herd will emerge.

One cannot but marvel at the boldness of the Indian who, leaning against a tree, calmly waits for the herd. Mosquitoes, in constantly increasing numbers, harass and sting him; he crushes them on his naked body, on his neck, on his legs; but the first rustle among the leaves finds him ready, motionless, his spear in his right hand. Sometimes he has to change his look-out post, to slip from one tree to another, until this sort of journey-by-guesswork through the forest brings him to the exact spot where the first wild pigs emerge, heavy-bodied, short-legged, snouts bent to the ground.

Trotting along, crushing the low vegetation, leaving a great dark trail behind them, they pass by unaware of him, absorbed in their own noise, in the blind self-confidence of the herd. After them come a few laggards, the dreamers. The hunter chooses his victim from among these, with one swift, sure glance. He lifts his spear to ear-level, aims accurately, strikes like lightning. The peccary falls, mortally wounded, and nothing stirs around the Indian, who remains unseen. The noise dies away. The stray pigs grow anxious, sniff to right and left and trot faster to join the rest of the tribe further on.

Without hurrying, the Jivaro goes up to the animal, which is already dead. He takes a creeper and binds the four paws together. He kneels down and, without an effort, hoists the heavy carcass over his shoulders, picks up his spear, and turns towards home. The sun is still high.

When he comes back to the hut, only the children will cluster round him, but next morning, while he holds his calabash of warm *awayusa* in his hands, he will tell the other men about his hunt and they will listen in silence.

Only the oldest of them will speak. He will give the commendation of the tribe: "*Mak' itei*... Well done!"

THREE : THE FISHERMEN

I

Naspak, the fisherman, generally uses a harpoon. At the end of a handle of light, porous wood, nearly six feet long, he fixes a tip of black *chonta* wood. A cable of plaited cotton is wound round the body of the harpoon and reaches to the tip. The weapon is laid in the front of the canoe.

The lagoons and rivers are well stocked with fish, but it is in the Rio Pastaza that most curious varieties are found, from the big *peixes* which are much sought after, lower down the river, by the people of Iquitos, to the electric fish whose discharge is dangerous. All are caught by the same method. A woman sits in the stern, the fisherman stands in the bow, upright in the sunshine. The skill and quickness of eyesight of the Jivaros are remarkable. Before we have seen a ripple of the surface of the grey or yellow water of the river, the harpoon has been thrown. They rarely miss their aim. The body of the weapon floats on the water and the cable unrolls swiftly. Two yards further on the fish, whose head has been pierced through by the tip, is seized. The fisherman breaks the slimy creature's neck with his teeth and throws it into the bottom of his boat.

Fishing is quickly over, for the Indian is familiar with the haunts of his favourite fish and with the nooks and roots where they hide at nightfall. He is satisfied with a small catch. His wives prepare it for his evening meal, grilled in a wrapping of leaves or boiled. Only when some festivity or revel is in prospect is fishing done on a large scale. In this case, the Indians use a venomous sap, known as *barbasco* in the civilized countries of South America and used under other names by all tribes of the Amazon.

On the eve of the chosen day, the creepers and roots that contain the narcotic are cut and brought home. Next morning they are prepared by the men, who crush them against the fire-logs, just as they do when preparing *natema* from *naegri* creepers. The fibres are collected into woven baskets, and loaded in a canoe. When the inhabitants of a hut go fishing with barbasco they divide into two groups. One group trails the basket along the river above a dam which the other group has prepared. The place chosen is a narrow one, where a strong current rushes through a screen of crossed bamboos against which the fish, stupefied or killed by the *barbasco*, are carried. They can be picked up by hand.

Men, women and children join in the sport. No need to bother about keeping quiet: the effect of the widespread narcotic is instantaneous. The small fish rise to the surface first; the bigger ones take longer to succumb and struggle against unconsciousness. But in a few minutes a fine catch is collected, among which, mingled with edible fish, can be found the notorious *piranhas*, the fish whose rapacity has helped to establish a proverb which says: "The Amazon carries no corpses."

II

Fred Matter, swimming in the lagoon, felt the disagreeable contact of a hard-scaled fish. He was naked; there lay the danger. The *canero*, a kind of sardine common in the basin of the Amazon was experimenting with him. This fish, which is extraordinarily inquisitive, tries to creep into the natural orifices of the body and eventually causes slight haemorrhages. These wounds, harmless in themselves, can bring death, for in a few seconds a horde of *piranhas*, attracted by the blood, rush on the man's submerged body and attack it everywhere. No amount of courage, no method of self-defence, can free the victim from these voracious creatures. In ten minutes the stoutest man is torn to shreds, devoured and swallowed.

But the *piranha*, called *pani* in Jivaro, has its use. Its jaw serves to cut arrows for hunting... A fair return.

III

Fish have their place in the witchcraft of the Amazon. Certain tribes of the Rio Napo invoke them in their incantations: the singing fish; the musical fish endowed with beneficient power; and the aphrodisiac *buffeo* found in the middle reaches of the Amazon.

The Jivaros, too, allow fish their place in the spirit world, but it depends on their weight and size. During the ritual fast for the enthronement of witch-doctors – and the fast which accompanies the shrinking of human heads – the active participants are allowed to eat only tiny fish, boiled. These, presumably, are harmless, on the reasoning that no spirit would choose such a form to be reborn into.

Among the beneficient fish in the Jivaros' canon is the water-boa, or anaconda, which is not uncommon in the lagoons and sometimes attains a length of more than 30 feet. The Jivaros never try to kill it. On the contrary, their attitude is one of respect and awe, for they share the belief, common to all the tribes of the Upper Amazon, that a man who disappears in a whirlpool is the chosen victim of the anaconda.

On the Napo, natives are afraid of being carried away while asleep on the shore, or while voyaging down the river in their canoes.

The water-boa is held to be endowed with a magic power which the witch-doctor invokes during his cures. The chief who directs the head-shrinking ceremonies counts on its support in his struggles against the *tunchi* – the dead man's magic breath. "I pour the boa's water," he says, filling the jar in which the trophy lies soaking.

I first met the water-boa near the small Potochi River in a region of dense forests, rivers overgrown with vegetation and short lagoons shadowed by trees. For long hours we had been hunting for the beginning of a track, for any sort of sign of life. There was nothing. We wandered on, amid that elaborately patterned scenery, sharing its silence.

Then I caught sight of a clearing. The current suddenly carried us towards it and as I stood up in the front of the canoe I noticed a tree whose bare trunk seemed to grow out of the river. Around it was wound what appeared to be a thick, glistening, clinging creeper, coloured grey and mottled with black. It was an anaconda and a splendid specimen. My oarsmen interrupted the rhythm of their paddles at the same moment as I aimed with the Mauser. I fired once, twice. It hurtled into the water a few steps from us and its mass as it fell set up a violent wash that prevented us from following its direction.

The Indians stayed motionless, silent with astonishment and shocked fear. I heard them muttering among themselves. Loosely translated, they were saying: "These pale faces have no respect for anything."

FOUR : WOMEN WITHOUT LOVE

I

The chief gave us the best proof of his confidence when he gave us the run of the hut during the men's absence. They had all gone off to hunt for turtles on the banks of the Pastaza; it was the laying-season. One morning they filled the canoes with big packets of *yamanche* done up in leaves and pushed their craft into the current. We waved to them from our camp; ten minutes later we landed near the hut.

Maceo, the witch-doctor, and the only man left among a dozen women, watched us coming without fear. Some time earlier we had shown him the curious colour-transformations of permanganate and had given him some with which to astonish his patients. Maceo was a cunning sorcerer and his presence made things easier for us with the women, although, indeed, we merely asked that they should carry on their usual occupations and let themselves be filmed.

For several days they went on chewing manioc, fetching water from the river, suckling their children and washing them, setting up their looms and using them, making baskets... All their activity was displayed before the eye of the camera while Guébriant and I covered whole sheets in our notebooks.

The Jivaro woman knows no leisure. From the time when, as a small girl, her share in games with boys consists in getting slapped, until the eve of her death, she never stops working and serving. The men's absence in no way lessens her activity, any more than it authorizes quarrels between the various wives of a single husband. On the contrary, they organize their lives in the best interests of the household. When one is pregnant, she takes over the easy tasks, looking after the fires and the children; the other women go to the plantation, paddle the family canoe, and clean the hut. One occupation, however, brings them all together: the preparation of *yamanche*. *Yamanche* is generally made with manioc, but it can include bananas or other fruit, such as *chontaruru* which, in the Jivaros' opinion and in my own, gives the best beverage. The roots are brought from the plantation in huge baskets, stripped of their bark and piled up in a big earthenware jar. After they have cooked for two hours they are left to cool. As soon as it is cool enough the women begin to chew big pieces of root. Often they get together in a group. Some sit near the jar that holds the mush, the others carry on their usual tasks. A single root is chewed on an average 35 times, taking about sixty seconds; then the masticated paste, soaked with saliva, is spat out into a huge receptacle set aside for the purpose. An old woman stirs the whitish substance with an *ipiako* – a sort of miniature paddle – and fermentation begins instantly.

The sight did not disgust us during the making of *chicha*, which is a cool and comforting drink; but the sight of the delousing process certainly disgusted us with the

women. They settled down comfortably in the sun and hunted their lice enthusiastically. They must have found it an easy task. Their sticky, unkempt locks – combs, like cosmetics, are reserved for the men – shelter generations of vermin. We were repelled by the ecstasy of the scratchers and their habit of eating the little creatures they dislodged. The session lasted as long as their appetites.

Occasionally the women felt the need to wash their hands. They drew up into their mouths as much water as they could hold and then spat it out gradually into their hands. They wash their children in the same way. I thought, not without regret, of European women who, by and large, are somewhat cleaner; but I was strangely moved by one Indian woman, the captive of an Achual warrior, whose cleanliness distinguished her from the rest; she did not spit or scratch herself continually, nor was she covered with ashes or incrusted dirt. My friends shared my admiration for this girl whom we called among ourselves "The Beauty". She had a fine skin, a charming profile and high, firm breasts, uplifted as she bore her water-pitcher on her shoulder. Not surprisingly, her husband was as jealous as any man can be.

The other female occupations are more normal. With a loom of primitive device they make loin-cloths, *itipi*, white for themselves and striped black and white for the men.

These pieces of cloth are somewhat coarse in texture but extremely strong and much treasured as heirlooms. "Not my father's loin-cloth!" was the shocked reply of an Achual when I offered him a pair of shoddy trousers in exchange for it.

Anklets and bracelets adorned with geometrical designs are made by the most skilful of the women; baskets of plaited fibre by the youngest.

The hardest part of an Indian woman's toil is in the plantations, for which she shares the responsibility with her husband. Carrying a child on her back, she digs five or six holes in the ground and sticks into each of them a cutting of manioc. Further on she repeats the process. Under a relentless sun she toils for hours, bowed down and heavily laden.

The Jivaro girl marries young. As she grows up at her mother's side she learns from her all that she needs to serve as drudge to the boys and later to her husband.

She reaches puberty at about twelve years old and although she is not allowed to take part in the feast of Kusupani – the feast of puberty – the news soon spreads throughout the region. Indians in search of a wife begin to visit her hut. They must win over the father by stories displaying their courage, their hunting prowess and the fame of their ancestors. The girl is hardly mentioned until the day when her father, deciding that such-and-such an Indian is worthy to be his son-in-law, gives her to him as a wife. Sometimes, among the Achuals, the future bridegroom brings an offering of feathers, particularly those of the white toucan. The marriage takes place without further ceremony than a general drinking-party. When the party is over, the couple go to some spot in the forest to consummate the marriage.

It is in the forest, too, that the woman bears her children. At the onset of her pains she leaves the hut, alone, and lies down in some previously chosen spot where she knows that her groans will not be heard in the hut. When the birth is over she immediately goes back with the newborn child and takes up her work again by the fireside.

It has been said that the men, meanwhile, utter cries and receive the encouragement of their friends. Actually, they lie quietly on their beds, ready to receive a son with joy and a daughter with disgust. It is all quite normal!

Relations between the sexes leave little room for gestures of affection. When the husband feels sexual desire he points out to his wife the path to the river and follows her there. Ten minutes later they return, she in front, he behind. But he does not always act with such modesty and, sometimes enjoys intercourse on his bamboo bed surrounded by the playing children.

Only during the great revels does the Indian express any sort of intimate feeling. When he is drunk he shows his clear preference for the woman who brings him the best *yamanche*. She is his choice for immediate pleasure, the other, or others, being destined for the blows which invariably wind up any good party. His wives accept favours and brutality with equal indifference; they are the two alternatives unalterably inherent in their condition. Nothing but the Jivaro's jealousy can create a more dramatic situation.

When a woman is chosen, she becomes bound by a chain of traditions and servile duties which she is as anxious as anyone to preserve. Her passivity and her fear of men may, on rare occasions, expose her to a sexual assault which is neither rape nor adultery, since she is essentially an apathetic partner.

The sexual act, devoid as it is of any sense of sin or magical significance, appears to her merely as a continuation of her household duties. She is, therefore, little inclined to indulge in it with anybody else than her lord and master. If she has been violated she will simply tell the incident to her husband. He will probably not hold her responsible, but the seducer will be lucky if he escapes from the husband's vengeance with his life.

Two Jivaro groups, the Huambiza and the Aguaruna, wage a furious vendetta against one another, the original cause of which was an abduction. The Huambiza, a tough race living in the relatively healthy district near the Cordillera, have among other Indians a reputation of being jealous warriors, well provided with wives. The headman has three or four, sometimes more. The Achuals, who are weaker and live confined to a more dangerous region, have few opportunities for jealousy and, consequently, for vengeance. Their women enjoy greater security and thus, I imagine, greater happiness.

One is forced to conclude that for the Jivaro woman, as for so many of her sex, happiness is of a purely passive order. Absence of feeling, lack of sympathy, indifference to pain – her own or that of others – restrict her to a complacent apathy.

In fairness, I must admit that once I heard an old mother crying as she nursed her dead child. But I remember also that her eyes were dry and that as soon as the time for ritual lamentations was over she laughed. It did not mean that she possessed an inhuman indifference. She was merely accepting her fate.

The death of a child does not leave an Indian mother shattered and despairing. There are no bonds between them of that kind.

Consider, for instance, the little girls who are carried about on their mothers' backs and tethered to them all day long by a wide strip of cotton. As soon as the children know how to imitate they know how to live, and the mother will stand aside without regret.

We must, however, distinguish between boys and girls. No mother would dare neglect a young male, or even to punish him. Indeed, among the Jivaros, there is nothing to punish a boy for. As soon as his little personality begins to assert itself all his wishes must be satisfied. Tradition demands it.

When children fall ill, it is never the mother's duty to look after them. She is held to be incapable of it; in the Jivaros' eyes she has no contact with the spirit world. Only the witch-doctor and the father can take charge. Often we saw the family procession climbing the slope up to our camp to bring us a child suffering from dysentery or fever. The woman held the tiny creature but when it came to carrying out the treatment we prescribed, the father alone was responsible. We used to watch a curious scene: a dignified Indian, painted and feathered, biting off half a capsule and spitting it into the mouth of an urchin whimpering in his arms.

In the huts, too, the father could be seen bending over the fire and inhaling the smoke to breathe it out afterwards over the chest of a child with a cough, or, in a serious case, covering him with ashes and vigorously massaging his body.

Because the mother is never allowed to perform the tasks that to Europeans would belong to her by right, our emotional response to the concept of motherhood is meaningless. These women know none of the conflicts that tear the hearts of our own mothers; they are deprived of those constant joys and pains that strengthen the natural bond. They need not be pitied, but they must be understood, these forest women whose only ends in life are procreation and drudgery. They are not even timorous. They are simply indifferent, matter-of-fact, living an animal existence which excludes devotion.

FIVE : A SACRIFICE AND THE SERPENTS

I

The Indians came back from the Pastaza with a load of great tortoises, smooth-shelled, waving their legs about in the bottom of the canoes. Not one had been wounded, for the Indian sport is to track them, pursue them and overturn them on the sand with one blow of the hand. The hunters have to be skilful to avoid being bitten, for the creatures' jaws, though toothless, are armed with a horny hide strong enough to break a spear. Amid cries of joy from the children the first tortoise was dismembered. Its paws were tied back with lianas and its white belly exposed for the sacrifice. The chief used a stone axe, brought from the Bobonaza, which made the tipping open of the carapace a long and painful affair. Fortunately, the tortoise can utter no sound. Gradually the carapace filled with blood, while the living flesh was torn asunder. The breast was laid over the fire and everything else, body and feet, cut up and put to cook immediately. The tortoise we carried back with us to the camp was treated in the same way, but before its death it yielded about a hundred eggs. We also got from it a good two pounds of dripping which, although somewhat rank in smell, enabled Guébriant to cook some manioc roots like chipped potatoes. That tortoise enriched our menus for a whole week. We ate tortoise soup, tortoise omelets, grilled tortoise. In the hut the women chipped away at the edges of the carapace, making the little tortoise-shell rings which they use to regularize their marriages.

During the past week the level of the river had sunk, disclosing palm-tree boles covered with silt and islands of mud, a favourite haunt of crocodiles. The air stank. A cloud of mosquitoes harried us so mercilessly from morning till night that we decided to set fire to everything around us. For two days, with the Indians' help, we built big bonfires at the foot of the nearest trees. On the third day we set them alight. It was a magnificent sight! Enormous flames rose torch-like into the blue morning sky, to die down only on the further side of the island. And while we stood motionless, watching this fire whose dimensions matched those of the country, the work of purification went on, dispersing or destroying the reptiles, spiders, mosquitoes and venomous vermin whose homes were there.

That evening, while going to the river to fetch water, Juan was bitten by a big green and yellow snake, the *loro matchako*. He did not die of it, but his cries of agony rang out for hours amid the dying flames of the conflagration. The spirits of the forest were having their revenge.

We were continually reminded of the dangers of the forest: the serpents, the trap-door spiders, the venomous ants, the eternal mosquitoes. We walked for hours through marshes, not knowing where we were going. We could face that, clad in our boots, stout shirts and caps. The forest has the right to defend itself and the animals that shelter within it have the right to live. I can quite see that I disturbed them with my weight and clumsiness. That was my risk.

But with our clothes off, the perils increased. One day Guébriant and Matter were scrubbing themselves in a cool stream while, further down, Ramon was washing his clothes. The weather was pleasant and not too hot. I arrived a little later, with my old cap on my head; it was lucky for me that I'd taken this precaution. As I was unbuttoning my shirt, a yellow snake reared up in front of me, its neck puffed out with fury from the resting place it had made in Jean's clothes, which were lying close by. I lashed at it with my cap and leapt backwards, but I had barely time to raise my stick before the reptile was on me again.

Snakes do not die easily. There were endless twists and turns among the long grass as I laid about me with my faithful stick, hitting random blows at the long, supple scaly body that moved so noiselessly. When it lay still at last, I grasped it near the head. The little carcass was still soft and clean. There was no blood, but when I passed my finger along its elastic surface I could feel hollows and bruises. I pushed open its jaws and saw its fine venom-fangs, sharp and delicately curved. With a piece of wood I stimulated the tips.

The amazing thing, as I explained to my friends that evening, was that I had felt no fear in the face of such danger. My reflexes had served me well. Yet at the Zoo, confronted with captive vipers caged and labelled, or with caymans lying inert in their concrete enclosures, I always experienced a feeling of repulsion and fear. Here, when we bathed in the lagoon, we gave no thought to the caymans. We had no intention of taking life too earnestly.

Ramon prepared the snake and hung it up in the hut to dry. Now it had its number and its name (*kaapi* in Jivaro). And now, hours after the event, I caught myself saying in horror, "I've had a narrow escape."

SIX : THE PROFESSIONAL SORCERER

I

The witch-doctor is the power of the Jivaros. He is the healer, the judge who condemns the guilty to death, the priest who brings comfort to the afflicted, the one voice in the tribe that cannot be disobeyed.

Maceo, the *wishin* of the tribe we lived among, was a conscientious witch-doctor and most accomplished. He could even draw the traditional figures of men and women and traced them with a firm hand on the paper I offered him.

He had been introduced to the spirit world by his father. During his long novitiate he had eaten the ritual meals of boiled manioc, *pachin* (small fish) and *kuillin* (small birds) which no other Indians will touch. Every evening he drank tobacco juice and the alkaloid *natema*.

He had learned to chant the invocations of the peoples of his tribe, who dwell on the banks of nameless rivers or of the single river they call Kanus, near the Cordillera. He had learned the secret of facial paintings, those mysterious patterns through which Indians and Spirits know one another.

One night, when he had learned all that needed to be learned, his father transmitted to him his magic power by breathing on his son's forehead. Henceforth, the sacred power, the *tunchi*, which works both good and evil, had permanently entered into him. Among the four or five fathers of families living in the hut Maceo alone possessed it. He was, so to speak, in a state of grace in respect of his relations with the spirits and, above all, by the way in which, deputizing for supernatural powers, he could affect the course of events. Thanks to the power that had been breathed into him his tribe was satisfied that he could influence a disease or, more precisely, comfort the sufferer. He could invoke the spirits of his ancestors to recognize and point out a guilty man. He could send forth the arrows of evil fortune (*wawik tsinsak*) or of good fortune (*pinger tsinsak*) – arrows endowed in each case with magic power. Thus he could assist his own group and instigate murders in enemy territory. His word was law and, in this respect, infallible.

His position in the tribe is envied by all his fellows. He need not hunt unless he chooses, nor work at reclaiming the soil nor at building and repairing his canoe. The group will provide for all his needs and that of his visitors, and they give him the finest gifts, and their most precious possessions.

And yet Maceo, and all the witch-doctors, are doomed. The Jivaros rarely make tribal war on each other – though they will attack white men or "foreign" tribes in strength. When evil falls upon them, or one of them is murdered, revenge is usually executed on the single person held to be responsible: the enemy witch-doctor. Thus Maceo knew that at any time – in a few days, perhaps – some far off *jivaria* might denounce him for a death or an epidemic. The tribe would build the war-barrier around the hut. Outside his enemies would lie in wait for him and he would leave his bed only under the protection of his wives. But no precaution could save him; his fate was inevitable. He would die. His head would be cut off and shrunk and this emblem of death without resurrection would be borne into the hut that had lain the curse on him.

The witch-doctor is often solely responsible for the murders and warlike excursions that decimate these tribes. They are not primarily motivated by a thirst for blood, although bloodshed is intimately connected with the tribal animistic tradition. The spirit world, death, murder, are the connecting links in a chain whose supreme power is known to the witch-doctor. When he condemns a man to death he is acting as high priest in a ritual sacrifice. He bears the condemned man no hatred – though hatred may animate the man chosen to commit the murder and the victim's relatives. Thus is fulfilled the fateful law that one must kill in order to live. All living creatures that dwell in the forest are subject to it, and the Jivaro above all. His enemies go with him everywhere; he guesses at their presence when he hunts or travels. He may not have seen the man-trap that will ensnare and cripple him, the *chuchupi* viper that pursues him relentlessly; but he walks through the forest aware of their imminence and he is afraid.

When night falls, the danger grows more distinct; evil spirits called *iguanchi,* in the shape of a monkey, black jaguar or puma, prowl round him as he sleeps. Cries ring through the darkness and sudden flashes, enlarged and transformed in his dreams, illuminate nightmare landscapes. Even we white men, with our efficient modern weapons and our lamps, could feel the menace of these nights; how much more violent, therefore, must be the anguish of an Indian whose life is constantly at odds with his environment. In his fear he will ask the all-powerful witch-doctor to overcome his dangers and confound his enemies. The men around Maceo had an utter trust in him which he could never betray.

II

A visitor, Chakae, came from his far-off hut beyond the Pastaza, in the land of the Maynas Indians, to be cured by Maceo of the syphilitic *pian*. In his own village every dwelling was surrounded by the *tanish* or war-barrier, for several witch-doctors had died.

But Chakae did not go straight to the sorcerer. First he put on a head-dress of red and black feathers, grasped his red-ringed staff in his right hand and went into the hut. In silence a woman brought him a stool and he sat down. His entry in no way disturbed the quiet activities of the group.

Baotista, his legs outstretched in the sun, was smearing poison over the tips of his darts and laying them out, fanwise, to dry. Vitiap was making a fine-toothed comb, with the neat gestures of an embroideress. The old chief spent a long time binding a ribbon (the *tsemat*) round his hair and fixing ornaments and artificial locks to his side tresses.

Not until he had completed his coiffure to the satisfaction of his children did he turn to the newcomer and speak a couple of words to him in a low voice.

Thus the visit began. Short sentences were spoken, their hands in front of their mouths, at first in whispers and then in increasingly loud tones. Quickly the conversation changed into a hurried dialogue, intoned to begin with and then shouted frantically. For a minute or two one of the partners would lead the discussion while the other emphasized each word with a vigorous "*Make!*" ("Good!") When his turn came to speak he outdid his predecessor in force and violence. We thought they were about to fight but they were merely exchanging the news of the day, telling one another about the good or evil fortunes of neighbouring *jivarias*. Mutual fear was the sole cause for this hubbub. Face to face and unprotected, they were indulging in these oratorical jousts with which warriors hearten themselves before battle.

"I'll convince you of my strength and courage!" said Chakae and indeed his upright staff looked more like a spear than an olive branch. However, their long-drawn-out vociferation finally pacified their excited nerves. This seeming fury, being shared, eased the tension and even led to friendliness. The two men merely made it a point of honour to prolong their altercation till they were exhausted. Then one of the chief's three wives brought vessels filled with the best *yamanche*. The reception ceremony was over.

Chakae now had the right to live in the hut. He went from one bed to the other greeting those he knew and resuming with them the traditional dialogue. Only now could he approach Maceo. Chakae's body was covered with reddish swellings, while the original sore had eaten deep into his right leg. He had come to ask Maceo to find the baneful dart in his wound and to cure him. A discussion took place on Maceo's bed, not so much to explain the disease from which Chakae was suffering – the cause of that was supernatural – but to decide what the medicine-man should be paid. They agreed on a short blow-gun of a type unfamiliar to the Achual but much sought after by the Maynas for hunting peccary, and Maceo agreed to heal him the following night.

III

To make contact with the spirits, Maceo had to enter into a trance by absorbing alkaloids or stupefacients, of which the two favourites were *maykua*, made of flowers crushed and diluted in water, and *natema*, obtained by a decoction of lianas. *Natema* is chosen for medical purposes.

Chakae went off alone, early in the morning, to cut a dozen pieces of the plant which the Jivaros call *naegri*.

When he returned he crushed them one by one against the fire-logs and threw them into a large jar full of water. The beverage simmered on the fire all day, concentrating its narcotic qualities. At nightfall it was collected in a half-gourd, or *tsapa*, which was carefully set down near the sick man's bed.

In the hut, the fires died down. The children stopped playing and lay down beside their sleeping parents. It was that uneasy time of night when all the forest insects blended their cries into one cry whose hallucinating shrillness echoed with equal intensity throughout the vast realms of darkness from the Cordillera to the ocean. The solitude would have seemed more haunting still had not the vampires, skimming around us menacingly, kept us on the alert. There was no sound in the hut.

Maceo rose and slowly drew near the sick man. He asked for the tobacco juice and his wife handed it in a boat-shaped vessel. Once more Maceo kneaded the moist leaves and, his head bent backwards, sniffed up the bitter liquid. I cannot describe the horrible throaty sound that suddenly broke the silence.

He repeated the process three times then, his hands outspread, he slowly spat out the tobacco, mingled with saliva. The long yellow thread of spittle hanging from his lips (and called *maer*) he slowly sucked back. Maceo performed this operation several times, as though to make sure it was working correctly, then he drew near the sick man and asked for the *natema*. It was brought him in his half-gourd and he drank it at one mouthful. A quarter of an hour passed while, seated on a stool, he began to mutter incantations. The woman fanned the sick man's body with a handful of palms. The incantations grew clearer as the narcotic began to take effect. Suddenly the song of healing broke forth. Bending over the sore, the witch-doctor shouted out the ritual words which were to give him greater power than any other magician, power over life and death. He had to find, within this festering sore, the evil charm in the shape of a dart cast by an enemy. Through his power he compelled beneficient spirits to come to his aid.

He sang:

"Wakani Wakani pasuk

Wakani pasuk

Timiano wi ermanke

Wi Wi Wi Wi..."

("Spirit, spirit of the spider, I am clothed and filled with thy spirit, I, I, I...)

The last words were repeated in the rapid rhythm induced by the *natema*. Immediately afterwards Maceo pressed his lips to the sore and sucked the pus greedily. He rose and tried to spit it out, mingled with tobacco. Maceo returned to the sick man and began his incantations once more:

"Kurishion Kurishion

Timiano Wi ermanke

Kurishion Wi ermanke

Wi Wi Wi Wi..."

("Little cantharides fly, I am clothed, I am filled with the cantharides, I, I, I...")

Unceasingly the palms waved over the head of the sick man, who was groaning as though in intolerable pain.

"Tawasamba timiano

Timiano tsingari

Tsingari wi ermanke

Wi ermanke

Wi, Wi Wi Wi..."

("I am crowned with a festal crown, I am clad, I am filled with it, I, I, I ...")

Maceo, quivering and foaming at the mouth, ceased his incantations and threw himself on the man's horrible wound. He was possessed by a frenzy, sacred or erotic. Suddenly he stopped, motionless as though at a climax of excitement. Then he rushed out of the hut. The sick man, sitting up on his bed, heard the witch-doctor's retchings. Then he beheld him returning, shattered but victorious, carrying the baneful dart.

The hut resumed its silence.

IV

Next day I looked at Maceo's ravaged face, his glittering eyes which shunned the daylight, and was deeply moved. And yet this exhausted man had been accustomed to alkaloids and stupefacients ever since the day, when, to celebrate his puberty, he had drunk whole jars of hot *natema*. I have seen children in a state of frenzy at the feast of Kusupani. I was told that some of them succumb to the drug and die a horribly painful death. But drinking *natema* can be pleasant when one is used to it. The chief often took it and, on such nights, a strange and gentle singing sounded from his couch.

What exhausts the witch-doctor is having to restrain his intoxication; his will to heal or prophesy is at stake. He cannot remain passive, as his invocations show. He is the interpreter of the spirits not by the miracle of inspired speech but because he wrests their power from them. Plants, waterfalls, shades of vanished creatures, the *Wakani* of his invocations, these strange creations of an inanimate world live again in his songs and are identified with him. He gives them life. Doubtless they remain mysterious to his patients and victims, but not to him, through whom they are revealed.

During the discussions held at dawn men will compare his powers with those of other witch-doctors. In the long run it is his personality that counts.

V

A long time ago – the *embuash* shrub, which provides the kapok with which Jivaros feather their darts, has since then flowered many times – an Indian from the north named Ossum came to seek out Maceo. "My wife," he said, "was planting manioc in a newly-cleared field. A monkey passed by among the trees and I followed it all day to kill it. When I got home I found nothing but the spoor of a deer. My wife had vanished."

Because the deer, *hapa*, is tabu to the Achual – the spirits of the tribal dead are believed to inhabit its body – the witch-doctor could not advise a punitive expedition against the animal. It would be better to use craft. While intoxicated with *maykua* he discovered a clever way to force the deer to give back the wife to her husband.

"Each morning," he ordered Ossum, "take a dish of fresh *yamanche* to the place where your wife was taken from you. Then wait; one day she will faithfully come back to you."

When the Indian got home he prepared the *yamanche* and carried it to his plantation. One morning he saw the deer coming towards him unafraid. The animal gazed into his eyes for a long time and then turned and went away. Ossum followed it. After a difficult journey through a low forest, the deer stopped at the foot of a hill on which stood a large hut. From afar off Ossum recognized his wife sitting with the family of a new master and sharing their food. He went back to Maceo and told him of the adventure.

"I knew the deer would show you the way," replied the witch-doctor. That night the spirits counselled war. The hunter Ossum was victorious and had the twofold joy of winning back his wife and slaying her. Since Maceo had given proof of his understanding with the spirits favourable to the tribe, his prestige grew accordingly. His fame spread to the far-off *jivarias* of Huasagua and the Capahuari.

It may seem strange that the Indian, who will not admit sickness and death to be natural phenomena but sees in them the manifestation of some magical and malevolent power, and who is therefore vitally interested in his witch-doctor's infallibility, should never blame the sorcerer for a failure. There are countless cases of fevers that have proved fatal, of wounds that have resisted the invocations of the medicine man. Prophecies as to the outcome of a war have been known to mislead Indians and make victims of the avengers. But these are cases of conflicting influences, where the magician's power, his *tunchi*, may have met a hostile *tunchi* that defeats it. The Jivaro accepts his fate without question through his greatness of soul and his sense of resignation that always makes him equal to his destiny.

SEVEN : THE AMATEUR SORCERER

I

One day – my logbook reminds me that it was August 25th, a Wednesday – I at last satisfied the longing that had possessed me and drank my first draught of the magic drink of *natema*.

It was the culmination of two curious days which began well, turned dangerous, brought violent sensations for me and ended, as they had begun, peacefully.

At six o'clock in the morning of the 25th, young Tsamarin, one of the chief's boys, ran up the slope leading to our camp. From far off he called out: *"Munti! Munti!"* – a word I had not noted in my questionnaire. Tsamarin pointed to my gun and, puzzled, I deduced that *"munti"* meant some animal – but what animal? An hour later it lay on our specimen-table. I was hot from racing past all the islands of the lagoon, but I was delighted. The *munti* is a blue night-bird with a wing-span of more than two yards. Its thread-like crest on a bony protruberance from a thick skull, the hooks on its wings, the absence of nictating membranes, all thrilled us as a new discovery. It is actually a rare bird, peculiar to the Amazon region, known as the horned *kamichi*. It lives near lakes, generally in pairs, but I hunted in vain for the female. It lives on a seed that Ramon calls *"lechuvilla"* and its flesh exudes an unpleasant smell. Our canoeists were also interested in the bird and told us that in Brazil the Indians crush its bones and mix them with the teeth of the *buffeo* to obtain an aphrodisiac powder.

After our lunch of oatmeal soup, grilled parrot, and tea, our friends from the hut brought us two Achual visitors, splendid types with impenetrable faces. Excited at the prospect of acquiring new data, I promptly got out my measuring kit, my card index, and the usual small presents – mirrors and reels of red thread – which were the reward for a session of measurement. Much tact was needed to persuade the younger Achual to sit down in front of me on a box and barely had the tips of my compasses touched his head when he rose and burst into a flow of invective of which I understood nothing. His companion leapt to his side and swore at me no less violently. The other Jivaros joined in and the noise was tremendous. Fortunately nobody was armed and we escaped violence, but we had to spend the whole day calming them down with sessions on the gramophone and with presents of canned food and thread. The imminent storm no doubt partly accounted for their highly nervous state.

At 6.30 p.m. we ate our supper of oatmeal soup, rice, jam and tea in the teeth of a horde of insects, cockroaches, mosquitoes and flies which swooped down on us in spite of our ingenious arrangement of lamps. At 7 o'clock we got under our mosquito-nets, sweating profusely. The rain could be heard some way off in the forest. Then it came down on us like an express train. We jumped out of our beds, pulled them into the middle of the hut and covered them with waterproof canvas. Ramon ran here and there collecting his birds while the three canoeists cowered among the cases.

We never knew what happened that night in the Indians' hut, but perhaps the thunder and lightning increased our prestige. At any rate, our two violent visitors of the previous day appeared at dawn and unhesitatingly sat down happily beside the packing-case. The chance was too good to be missed, and we did our job swiftly in spite of weariness. We even succeeded in buying from them the snake-skin bracelets they wore on their wrists and some magnificent bamboo ear-ornaments that hung from their mutilated lobes.

After our daily hunt on the lagoon, we went back to the hut and found them half-drunk with *yamanche* and quite devoid of dignity. A general revel was being organized in their honour in which everybody, even the children, took part. I might have joined in, but I was absorbed in watching the preparation of *natema*. A one-eyed Indian who had recently arrived from Huasaga (three days' journey on foot, in the south) supervised the cooking of the lianas and, without leaving his fireside, poured water into the jars from time to time.

His wife was ill with fever. She was a handsome creature despite her yellowish skin, and I would have liked to give her a few tablets of quinine sulphate to relieve her. But her husband, beside whom I sat down, had more faith in the witch-doctor. He ate my tablets himself and, finding them bitter, spat them out in disgust. Then he pointed to the liquid simmering on the fire:

"*Natem! pinger natem!...* Good *natema*," he said.

His ruse was somewhat clumsy, but I was careful not to thwart him. For several days I had been waiting for an opportunity to partake of the magic drink. What I had managed to pick up from the sorcerer during his delirium and hallucinations did little to enlighten me as to their nature. What psychological and sensorial disturbances take place? Does it make you see visions and, if so, what sort? Do you hear noises? What sort of noises?

The worthy Ramon, who claimed to have taken *ayaguasa* (a drink similar to *natema*) hundreds of times, gave me abundant information.

"The first time," he said, "it was on the Rio Napo; I was ill, *fui enfermo*, horribly ill. The next time I was ill, but rather less so; just for one day. The third time I enjoyed *ayaguasa* very much. It was like going to the pictures – *como el cine*."

Juan, the *boga*, who had become attached to me – no doubt to try to make me forget his immense laziness – strongly disapproved of dreams and ecstasies. He was convinced one died of them. The other two oarsmen, Isidro and Santo, practised witchcraft in their own tribe on the Bobonaza; they were therefore well acquainted with the effect of the drink, but would reveal nothing.

The uncertainty and the desire to test my white man's strength against the Indian drug impelled me to accept the one-eyed Jivaro's offer. I would drink natema that night. Matter and Guébriant agreed to stay with me in the hut, mostly out of friendliness, a little in order to study my reactions.

Night fell. Maceo drew near me and handed me the cup full of *natema*. Everybody watched me as I drained the bitter drink at one draught. "Now," said the *boga* Juan, "lie down." I obeyed. After a quarter of an hour, I bent towards him as he sat at my feet.

"Shut your eyes and keep still," he commanded.

His voice sounded strangely soft and drawling, as though I were under chloroform. A conviction of extreme weakness – a fear hitherto unknown to me – seized me and forced me to open my eyes. All the fires were out in the hut. A thick, impenetrable blackness overwhelmed me and filled my field of vision. Suddenly an enormous flame shot through it. A crowd of new sensations harried me, all disagreeable and soon agonizing. My heart seemed to thump louder every second, my temples throbbed rapidly and painfully.

I could hear Guébriant saying: "Your pulse is normal," but when I tried to sit up and answer him my head felt so heavy I could not raise it from the bed. My hands, on the contrary, felt far too light and out of control.

A violent hiccup shot me to the edge of the bed. Somebody put a lemon into my mouth and I began a series of vomitings that went on for four hours. From time to time images appeared, without order or coherence: enormous dogs' heads, Indians armed with spears lying in wait for me in the forest, gigantic spiders.

I tried to escape, to fight against them – or it so seemed to me in my delirium. Actually, cold and numb, I kept repeating the single phrase: "Oh Lord, how revolting!"

I could hear my companions discussing whether an injection of morphine would help and Juan recommending a second cup of *natema* but, isolated in my ravings, I could show neither my terror nor my will to extricate myself from it.

At last dawn brought me relief, I left the hut and threw myself down in a copse, groaning and shivering with cold. Guébriant, who had followed me, wrapped me in a blanket and led me gently back to the hut, disgusting object that I was.

This deplorable experiment, which proved nothing but the efficient functioning of my stomach, won me special consideration from the Indians. They had been through these torments themselves at their first attempt. The chief himself brought me a cup of hot *awayusa*, the only drink I could tolerate that day, and the rest of the tribe were as eager to please us as, the previous day, they had been irritable and ready to take offence.

Matter was able to film the various stages of making a jar, from the first blending of the clayey soil, flue, with crushed charcoal, *maschin*, until the firing of the vessel. The old female potter even obligingly exposed her flat bosom to the sun, whereas all the other women were careful not to let their shadows cross the field of the picture. Several times during the day the chief sat down beside me on the bed where I was painfully sleeping off the previous night's intoxication.

Such widely differing attitudes can only be explained by the sensitiveness of primitive beings, always on their guard, anxious to maintain an equilibrium which is constantly shifting in their disfavour. While preparing my instruments I must have made some gesture which offended and seemed to threaten them. They had not tried to understand. How could they, deprived of any means of comparison? It was fear alone that awoke their resentment and might, if we had been unlucky, have led them to kill us; but the new day had wiped out fear and we were friends.

EIGHT : THE WAR DANCE

I

The chief looked at the swarm of ferocious flies and said calmly: "Tomorrow, many men will come."

I do not know how he connected the flies with the arrival of visitors, but next day we heard the shouts that form part of the traditional welcome, and they were so numerous that we decided to visit the hut.

Four Indians had just come in, four fine Indians whose long, black hair, tied back like horses' tails, and brown loin-cloths, showed they had come from far. They carried in their hands the heavy *chonta*-wood spears that are used in war. No women were with them. Our presence puzzled them, for they cut short the ceremonial part of the visit and the chief passed round *yamanche*.

We appealed to the chief and the witch-doctor for enlightenment. Who were these men? Why had they come? The evasive reply was that these men had travelled for more serious reasons than the pleasure of the journey. We could learn those reasons if we would agree to lend our arms to three inhabitants of the hut whose skill at hunting was known. We agreed. Ramon went to fetch three rifles (unloaded) and, for safety's sake, pistols for ourselves (loaded). When the three natives were armed they were joined by Baotista, who owned a Winchester dating from the rubber-trade era, and the four men lined up facing the visitors outside the hut.

The war-dance, the *Neymartin*, began.

"*Neymartasin Winaie*. I come to dance *Neymartin*," chanted the visitors, raising their spears and swaying rapidly from one foot to the other. The men of the hut waited opposite them, their guns on their shoulders.

"I have come to fetch you to fight beside me," chanted the visitors.

Our Indians began to dance, raising their spears and chanting with their hands before their mouths: "I have already fought."

The dance went on, each group speaking in turn:

"*Amue okamue*. Do you seek me?"

"*Nanki sorusta*. Give me your spear."

"*Nanki susaie*. I give you my spear."

Suddenly the chanting stopped. Smiling, the warriors went back into the hut where the women offered them fermented drink. The hut life became normal. The mothers put the children to sleep, huddled up in their short fibre hammocks; the men lounged on their beds, except for Kuhi, who was busy hollowing out the inner tube of his new blow-gun.

Puzzled, but persistent, we gradually dragged the truth of the matter from these secretive creatures. It required patience, then bold questioning and then more patience, with long sessions beside Maceo's bed.

The Indians had come from a hut in the north, five days' journey upstream. They were pure-blooded Achual, who lived in a constant state of vigilance and tension. Their headman had sent them in search of allies and they had come from so far away because all the Jivaro communities of the Upper Pastaza were hostile to them, and they could count on support only from the tribes living on the left bank, the Maynas and the Siguin. It revealed a strange blend of friendship and hatred within one tribe, a real political struggle, and the protagonists reasoned like civilized beings. Why they needed reinforcements was difficult to discover, but at last we found out that they had killed a witch-doctor on the Bobonaza river and the murderer was hiding in their hut, which was already preparing to withstand an attack.

II

Maceo, having drunk *maykua* and taken the advice of the spirits on the possible issue of a war, came out of his trance to report a favourable answer and, their mission completed, the four visitors prepared to leave next morning.

That evening I told my friends I was anxious to go along with the Indians to their *jivaria*. I asked them to carry on with the work in the Siguin district and look after the camp, our apparatus and our collection in my absence. I had some difficulty in persuading Matter and Guébriant, who were as keen as I on the adventure, but finally we divided the party into two groups. Ramon, the *boga* Juan and I were to leave for the north next day.

There was no opposition from the Jivaros and at dawn, in a thick mist, I embarked in the Indians' big canoe, taking only my rifle, my Colt revolver, a small first-aid kit and presents for barter.

We sailed rapidly down the Siguin, though we had to cut our way with machetes through a tangle of dead trees and floating branches, and at the river mouth, despite the speed at which we were travelling, Juan harpooned a big flat fish which formed the mainstay of our food supply during the journey.

As soon as the river Pastaza was reached, we began the slow journey upstream, hugging the bank. The men used their poles; every yard meant a considerable effort. The violence of the current forced us into wide deviations under the dense foliage of the banks or near the shore. These were the most pleasant moments, for they enabled us to walk on hard sand and dig up tortoise eggs. The Jivaros went on punting in silence with their flexible poles; they would stop for a moment to drink *yamanche* or to listen to the distant howlings of a wild dog, and then push off again.

Our first night on shore was made hell by the ceaseless ferocity of the mosquitoes.

The Indians stoked up the fire, but all measures were useless and in the small hours of the morning, drenched with sweat and feverish from their bites, I gave the word to start off again.

The sun soon dispersed the painful memories of the night, and the day ran its unvarying, monotonous course. About midday I shot two parrots for our evening meal, two fine red and blue *aras* which were darting over the wide river bed.

When the second night fell we went on. We did not rest but pressed on without a halt. The Jivaros were anxious to pass Chambira in the darkness. We had to keep along the left bank, where the current was particularly strong. Progress was so slow that the mosquitoes flew alongside and stung us with unimaginable fury. At dawn, behind a bend that hid us from sight of the *pueblo*, the Indians halted, exhausted. They had been paddling without respite for over 20 hours. We made a fire in a dampish thicket and after a meal of fish and a banana set off again, strengthened. Luckily we now came to a succession of sandy islands which enabled us to stretch our legs and lighten the canoe. At last, as rain was threatening, we put up a little shanty to sleep in. As we lay down we felt that all the storms of the tropics might fall and soak us and destroy our frail palm-leaf roof. We did not care. We were too weary. Sleep was all we wanted.

Next day we reached the narrow mouth of a river that Juan called Rio Tunegrama. We went up it as far as its first bend, in deep shade. The trees met overhead and the leafy vault gave the river a sinister, theatrical appearance. Suddenly the forest seemed further off; for more than 100 yards the ground was covered only with shrubs or young, widely-spaced trees. We landed. Juan said there had once been a village of Chimikae Indians here; missionaries had visited it and built a chapel – there was even talk of buried treasure. Undoubtedly the place had once been inhabited. I saw foundation posts in sufficient number to reconstitute the elliptical shape of a few huts.

Not without pride, one of the Achuals spread out his arms and told me: "The Jivaros destroyed it all."

We spent the night on a mound from which the long grass had been cleared. There were fewer mosquitoes, but instead we had to defend ourselves against vampires of incredible audacity. Their bite is never fatal, but it has to be avoided as these pernicious creatures recognize and pounce on the victim who has already been sucked by them. Half asleep, I felt them approach my hands and face, but fortunately the slightest gesture drives them off.

Next morning, after a plentiful draught of *yamanche*, we set forth again. The river soon grew narrow, wandering among fields or rushes or becoming suddenly congested between two walls of impenetrable forest. In the late afternoon we reached a calmer stretch, with muddy banks. The Indians moored the canoe to a branch and signalled to us to get out. We had to make our way through the forest.

The following night was one long struggle against an invasion of great ants that stung most cruelly. My beard was full of them. Ramon groaned for hours on end, tossing and turning on his bed of damp leaves. In the morning we were shocking sights, weary from lack of sleep, in agony from the ant bites and in no shape to battle through a forest in which there was no clear path. The only guides for our stumbling steps were a few marks on the trees and occasionally a short stretch of trampled undergrowth. But the Achuals, leading the way with swift, supple strides, never hesitated.

Several times we had to cross torrents, using tree-trunks as bridges. I was forced to tie my boots round my neck and walk across like a tight-rope artist, using my rifle to try to keep my balance.

Suddenly, at a gesture from the man in front, our procession stopped. In the topmost branches of a tree a little ahead of us I made out a brown, motionless form. It was a monkey, a fair-sized *kotto*. Quickly I went up to an Achual, who was already preparing his dart, and made him understand that I wanted to shoot. I aimed with my Colt. One shot, two shots... The reports scared the Indians but the monkey kept quite still, hanging up there on his branch with his head turned towards me.

An Achual came up, pulled a dart from his quiver, rolled up a tiny wad of cotton near one end of it, fixed in the poisoned tip, pushed the dart into the tube of the blow-gun, put it to his lips and blew violently. The dart hit its mark. I saw the monkey pull it from his wound, but he could not reach the poisoned point which had broken off in his flesh. A minute later he fell, his limbs rigid. The Indians whooped for joy. When I examined the body I found that my two bullets had indeed pierced the animal's breast, but without the effect of the poison he would not have fallen for several hours.

The Jivaros tip their darts with *curare*, which they obtain by barter from the Indians of the Lower Marañon. The only preparation peculiar to the Jivaros – and even then it is not in common use – is the juice of certain large ants (*mumatatchi*) extracted by slow cooking and added to the poison to strengthen it.

Thanks to this *kotto* we now had a slightly more varied diet than the over-fermented *yamanche*. Juan quickly made a fire beside a stream. Water was boiled in a jar that had held manioc paste and the monkey was hung up by the feet over the fire. When all its fur was singed, the skin was scraped off with a machete and the flesh cut up. The pieces are usually boiled, but I tried grilling my share over the flames. It was not a success. It rendered the meat positively uneatable.

The forest grew so dense that we could advance only when bent double. It seemed to me that we were going uphill, but I could not be sure. Weariness bewildered me. Yet we pressed on. The dread of another night on that putrid soil gave us all renewed energy.

At the end of the day we crossed a clear, playful little torrent into which I plunged up to the neck, revelling in its cool relief. On the further side, on a hill that had been cleared, stood a hut.

It was journey's end.

NINE : DISARMED BY THE JIVAROS

I

The hut was a huge one: 28 yards by 18 yards. Twelve outside supporting posts, seven interior supporting posts and four strong stakes in the centre of the house held up a palm-leaf roof. The family circle was quite a clan: more than 15 bamboo beds, with a fire burning in front of each.

A dozen paces away from the hut, exactly following its oval shape, stood the protective war-barrier, a stockade nearly 7 feet high made of a series of light, slender tree-trunks (*tundana*) of equal size, bound together by thick lianas and strengthened by cross-pieces. The wall secured them against enemy attacks, and only two narrow openings at the two ends allowed passage in and out of the enclosure.

The Indians had been warned of our arrival, probably by the drum, a tall piece of wood pierced with two apertures which relays messages across incredible distances. One of the Achuals, to whom I had taken a liking because of his youth and his courage on the difficult journey, led me to the chief, an aged man, who gave me a long look straight in the eyes. I noticed a big scar on his chest and I went close and touched it with my finger.

"*Make!* Good!" I said, holding out my hand to him.

He was pleased with this direct approach, for he ordered his wives to bring me some *yamanche*. Immediately a number of Indians gathered round and began to behave as all these native do: feeling my boots, putting on my cap and rubbing their hands on my beard. My short hair and bristly chin amused them inordinately, and surprised them far more than the colour of my skin (they must have thought I was ill). A general distribution of thread and mirrors finally put them all at their ease. The women rose from their hearths and drew near, stooping low. But the excitement soon died down; the more urgent interest of fear overrode all else.

Next morning the atmosphere in the hut had changed for the worse. At dawn, in spite of my stiffness and the cold mist that filled the hut, I drank *awayusa* with the Indians. Nobody spoke and I lay down again on my bamboo bed, feet to the fire. Daylight brought rain, which kept most of the men indoors. I went from bed to bed, drinking a mouthful of *chicha* each time and beginning a difficult conversation. Today there was a barrier between us, an underlying hostility. But I persevered. I wanted to make friends with them, but also to carry away as many objects as possible, for these Indians were better workers than those of the Siguin. Not one was idle. Some were cutting darts or paddles, others using balls of cotton to clean the incredible rifles they had acquired by barter. Many were armed, some with old Winchesters with rotten butts which they showed me proudly. I counted twelve fire-arms, which is unusual among creatures so completely out of touch with the outside world. Perhaps allied tribes to whom they had appealed for help had sent them their best warriors and their weapons. Certainly there were more men than women-a fact that confirmed my conjecture.

My first duty, according to Ramon, was to show my arms. The chief tried them out himself and the recoil of the Colt produced its usual effect. The pistol disappointed him, but this personal opinion did not prevent him from demanding it as well as the rifle.

"Weapons! Quick, weapons!" he demanded, his face threatening. At his words the hostility burst forth into the open and his warriors surrounded him, staring at us with enmity.

The Achual who had introduced me to the chief insisted that I would get the guns back later, but I wanted to argue. How could we escape alone, with no guide, through an unknown forest where we would be at the mercy of our pursuers, without weapons? But Ramon counselled caution. To argue now, he said, was to invite immediate murder. We were, of course, heavily outnumbered and though we might shoot a few down the others would soon overwhelm us.

Resignedly I handed the weapons over, keeping on my face the pleasant smile which I had schooled myself to maintain always when in the presence of the natives.

The smile hid acute distress. Not since the expedition had begun had I passed a more unpleasant moment. I was not frightened but, separated from my friends, I could not help remembering the legends and stories of the fate of other explorers. The situation was undoubtedly alarming.

Ramon and I decided that we must stay awake at all costs and keep together to avoid being surprised one by one while sleeping. We also decided to continue to hand out presents; it seemed safer to possess nothing that would arouse the Jivaros' envy. But once our meagre plan of action had been settled, I took full advantage of the freedom to move about that the natives granted us.

The hut was in a state of war. All activities were devoted to transforming it into a fortress. The women went to the plantations each morning to bring back big supplies of manioc and plantains which were promptly masticated and placed in store against a siege. The men, as soon as the torrential rain had ceased, went down to the river to fell trees suitable for fire-logs. The hunters brought back a number of monkeys, tied together by their tails round a stick. Most of them were the species called *makisapa*, of which they relished the tender meat and the brains. The children, infected by the excitement, imitated their parents' war-dances and practiced spear-throwing.

In the evening, while exploring outside the war-barrier, I discovered an improvised hut under which stood a strange piece of apparatus: four branches, laid crosswise, supported a tree trunk, skilfully cut off at the ends, measuring six and a half feet by two feet six inches, stripped of its bark and hollowed out. At nightfall an old woman brought a brand and some branches and lit a fire just below the tree trunk. The cries of grief she uttered as soon as the flames rose told me that a corpse was lying in this wooden coffin. The loud lamentations attracted nobody and the old woman remained alone, crouching before the fire until it died down, when she rose again.

The funeral rites of the Jivaros, which are not complicated, yielded further proof of the family discipline of these tribes. The right to preserve the body of a dead man belongs exclusively to his relatives. As soon as these primitive beings notice that the corpse is rigid they prepare the tree trunk in which it will lie for five or six months. The coffin is hollowed out with a stone axe and with fire, at great speed. The Jivaros dread the sight of a dead man. The corpse is laid out on its back in the hollow and hidden by a cover which exactly fits the opening and is nailed down with thin slips of *chonta* wood. Every night the mother comes to weep and light the ritual fire until the time when the witch-doctor unfastens the coffin and discloses a dead man whose evil power has completely disappeared. In these parts decomposition does not take long, and when the body has become a skeleton the bones are put into a great jar and taken inside the hut. If the dead man is endowed with considerable beneficient power, his relations carry him along with them when they travel by river and do not even abandon him when, for one reason or another, they change their home.

Sometimes, while examining the big earthenware pots that stand on the bamboo shelf in all Jivaro huts, I have laid my hands on skulls in a fairly good state of preservation, but I never managed to take one away.

Again, one day, when I was digging under the base of an abandoned hut in the Katirpesa, near our base camp and south-west of the Santiago river, I found a whole skeleton. As I began to remove the bones, two Indians emerged. They had been watching my actions for a long time, and they put back one by one into the grave all the bones I had taken out.

Bodies buried in this fashion are those of orphans or unimportant people. Headmen and magicians, when they avoid having their heads cut off – which is unusual – and die of old age, are buried in the middle of the hut. A few sticks are planted over their heads and the whole group emigrates.

We feared that the hostile attitude of the Indians towards us might, by some queer logic, be dictated by the death of the man over whose body the old woman was making hasty lamentations and we watched every move with wary keenness.

After a frugal evening meal of manioc and small boiled fishes, the women stoked and fanned the fires so that their flickering light shone continuously through the hut and set ghostly shadows moving against the roof. At each gateway of the enclosure two warriors stood with guns. Some of the Indians went out, preceded by their wives, and came back soon afterwards, unhurried. Contrary to the custom in other huts, the children went early to bed and the men talked from one bed to another. Three of them were swallowing great quantities of *natema*. They were witch-doctors. Two were in the prime of life, but with deeply wrinkled faces, the third was quite young, a novice still wearing his long hair loose on his shoulders. The drug produced a ludicrous effect on him, and as he was forced to drink a fresh draught he moaned: "*Nuha, nuha!*" But the women he was calling to his aid merely laughed at him and pushed him aside.

Although several warriors were lying side by side in some of the beds, one bed remained unoccupied. The magicians pulled up their seats alongside and settled down, burying their faces in their hands. Excitement overwhelmed them and incoherent speech flowed from their mouths. They seemed a prey to the deepest despair, wringing their arms and falling on their knees. The chief joined them, and he too, moaned and babbled.

This convinced me that the empty bed had belonged to the dead man. These trances probably accompanied invocations to his spirit for I heard the word "*wakani*" repeated continually. Ramon and I expected the worst and had kept our boots on and made a plan of escape. We would race across the 15 yards that separated us from the nearest opening and, if we got past the guard, somehow get down to the river, swimming and running. Juan was sitting near the door, already on the alert, his fibre blanket wrapped round him.

As the drink began to take effect the natives' hostility deepened. Their faces looked threatening and every time they passed by they jostled us without respect. Not until the night was well advanced and the drink had begun to make them tipsy did they begin to relax their attentions.

At dawn their intoxication was almost complete. They were staggering about from one end of the hut to the other. As I watched hope began to burn again in my mind. Suppose I could recover our guns! It would be terribly risky, but if it succeeded it would put an end to this harrowing uncertainty, this continual waiting to be butchered or to be on the run, helpless and unarmed.

I made up my mind. The rifle and the Colt were lying on the chief's bed, behind the sleeping bodies of his two wives. Calmly I rose from my stool and, on the pretext of wanting to relieve myself, strolled quietly towards the palisade. As I returned into the hut I paused by the chief's bed and, bending down, deliberately seized the guns. The rifle I passed at once to Ramon; the Colt I kept in my hand as I fastened the cartridge bag to my belt.

Now I could act with confidence. I felt safe with my Colt again in my hand and was quite prepared to shoot down the first Indian who attacked me.

Their immediate reaction was one of stunned surprise, but they took no hostile action; they were still under the influence of the drug and went on staggering round the hut in a ring, jerking their limbs like puppets. I remember thinking that it was queer behaviour for men in danger. If their opponents suddenly materialized outside the war-barrier they would go down before them like skittles.

Armed again, we could carry out our escape plan, but it was still too dark to give us much help and we resolved to take a chance and stay in the hut until the first strong rays of sunlight pointed out the path to the river. As we waited some of the Indians, who had slept the whole night through wrapped in their blankets and oblivious of the noise of the revellers, awoke and rose from their beds. Seeing us sitting on our stools, armed, they went to the headman and questioned him in a series of excited speeches interspersed with threats towards us. Some even went so far as to seize the butt of my pistol but I drove them away. All the while I did not cease to smile. To act the simpleton is the best defence against these people who are not deeply cunning and quite ignorant of our art of lying.

My confident air discouraged their hostility and made them amenable to parley, but their efforts to persuade me to surrender the guns broke on my stubborn resolve not to do anything of the sort. Confused, and robbed of the advice of the headman who was now lying completely unconscious beside his wives, they did not know what to do, except talk They talked a great deal but at last, as if wearying of the parley, a number of them took up their blow-guns and quivers and went off hunting Among them was my young fellow-traveller, the Achual who had introduced me to the chief. As he passed by I explained that I was anxious to return to the Siguin, as we had agreed. He refused angrily and walked out.

The hut was now almost empty. The drunken witch-doctors had joined the headman in drugged slumber. The remaining natives had lost interest in us. The time had come.

Calmly, Ramon, Juan and I walked towards one of the openings in the war-barrier. As we reached it a warrior stepped forward to bar our way. We pushed him aside and, taking to our heels, raced towards the path that led into the forest. Behind us shouts rang out, but there were no shots.

I will not dwell on the return journey to the Siguin. There was a long trek through undergrowth in an exhausting atmosphere. Rain fell incessantly. The soggy earth gave way beneath our feet. On the alert, keeping watch all day and all night, halting at every sound, we at last reached the navigable part of the river.

The canoe had disappeared, as we had feared. As we stared in dismay at the empty river Juan stepped into the breach and saved us as he had already saved us many times during the forest trek. Without him to guide us on the forced march we should have lost ourselves or fallen into the hands of Indians and now, when it looked as though we must perish among the undergrowth, he set out alone to seek the boat. At last he found it, cleverly camouflaged, more than half a mile up the branch of a river.

In frantic haste, paddling with all our might, we fled towards the river Pastaza and our base camp on the Siguin.

TEN : FRANCESCO THE AVENGER

I

Overjoyed, we saw at last the sunny shores of our lagoon and Isidro waving to us from our hut. It was noon. Matter, Guébriant and Santo had gone off by canoe to explore the farther side of the lagoon and had left behind them two new lodgers in their stead: two fine caymans, nearly but not quite dead, tethered to the posts of the house. The gaping wounds in their heads did not reveal which weapon, spear or rifle, had been used to strike them down.

The reptiles had been struggling there for two days, waiting for Ramon to despatch them with knife and arsenic. In fact, he used chisel and hammer.

A few hours later, Matter and Guébriant clambered up the slope, Fred, naked to the waist as usual, carrying his camera on his shoulder; Jean wearing his everlasting straw hat. Behind them the grinning Santo brought up the paddles.

We hoisted the Tricolour to celebrate our reunion and, in honour of the splendid dinner Ramon was preparing, we endeavoured to trim ourselves up. Out came razors and clippers and we sprinkled ourselves with camphor spirit before putting on our clothes, which the humidity had not yet rotted. Cleaned up, the hair on our now close-shorn heads smoothed into order, we played at being the perfect explorers of popular tradition. Thanks to civilization – our civilization – we could still appreciate such conventions as shaving soap and dry trousers. They even helped us to forget the anguish of the previous day – an anguish in which Fred and Jean had shared.

Matter and Guébriant, indeed, had experienced some anxious days. The rain, which had not ceased, kept them in camp. At first the Indians came to see them only after the day's hunting, to ask for tins of food or exchange feathers for thread, but one morning, five days after I had left, Kuhi, the chief's brother, came running up. He climbed up to the raised floor and said excitedly: "Enemies are coming to attack us."

"What enemies ?" asked Matter.

"Muratos," Kuhi answered, and burst into a long speech, emphasizing his words with violent gestures. From this torrent of words Fred and Jean gradually winnowed a few facts. That day, at dawn, hunters had appeared who were not of the tribe. More exactly, traces of men who were certainly not Jivaros had been found. Kuhi had first made the discovery; then one of his wives, who was paddling his canoe, had seen them; then the chief, finally the whole hut. To confirm this disquieting news, about 20 Indians swarmed into our camp and settled down on our beds and boxes with the obvious intention of staying there.

Matter and Guébriant, not wholly satisfied, debated among themselves. How much reliance could be placed on Kuhi's word? Why had the Indians vacated their own hut to rest in ours? Were they waiting to be attacked in our hut or was it a ruse to try and throw their enemies off the scent?

They were still discussing how much trust could be placed in Kuhi when the Indian, speaking for the whole crowd, demanded arms for self-defence.

Their ruse was now so obvious that Jean and Fred felt inclined to treat the whole incident as a joke. The fact is that Indian tribes are so exceedingly prudent that none will venture into open territory when they have decided to undertake a warlike expedition. Further, no genuine threat of war can remain secret from the threatened tribe. A wonderful system of news transmission, of which we were ignorant at the time, enables the huts to communicate with one another across miles and miles of virgin forest. War-drums serve as telegraph wires. If the Muratos, who lived nearly 200 miles to the south in the great islands of the Rimachi lagoon, had ever thought of making war on the Achual Jivaros, they would never have picked out these living on the banks of the Siguin, who were poor and had few women to steal. Moreover, they would have had vast stretches of forest and marshland to cross, in the midst of which the Jivaros had built look-out posts which nothing could escape.

But a real danger to the white man often lies behind the incidents which seem merely farcical. Matter and Guébriant knew the fate of the Scandinavian and American expedition which had settled on the banks of the Upper Morona, about 50 miles west of our camp. After a month or two of friendly relations with the Huambiza Jivaros, some blunder had aroused the hostility of the tribe. Of the nine men who had left Cuenca three or four months earlier, only three came back, and in a state of utter exhaustion. Jivaro spears had destroyed their six comrades.

With these memories in mind, Jean and Fred were determined to give the Jivaros no opportunity for attack. While Guébriant tried to convince the chief of his goodwill and promised to be his ally, Matter filled the spare chambers of the pistols and passed one to Jean. Seated on cases and leaning against the bamboo wall, they stayed motionless all day. Santo, trembling, brought lunch, and the chief was invited to share it. But, though he. was passionately fond of tinned sardines, he only glowered angrily.

By the end of the day the two captive and unwilling hosts had decided to defend themselves energetically and to liquidate as many as possible of their guests. I know the feeling; your nerves are on edge from the monotony of the daily effort and the exhausting climate, and, suddenly confronted with concrete and urgent danger, you welcome the opportunity to assert your strength. During certain hours of danger I have laughed for sheer joy, glad of an open threat and even hoping for the worst. You want to be revenged for the long drawn-out loneliness, the uncertain noises, the unexplained howlings, the uncommunicative faces and the mysterious words. You reach the stage when it becomes essential to press the trigger. I am convinced that, even in face of certain death, this impulse of release would be irresistible.

No attack came. The resolute attitude of Jean and Fred, together with the powerful impression that their irrevocable decision had left, worried the Indians considerably. Towards the end of the day, Kuhi left first, his wife paddling his canoe. They passed in front of the camp and disappeared for a few minutes behind the thick water plants. When he reached home he gesticulated joyfully to the rest of the men in our hut: a gesture which said that the Muratos had fled. One by one, in dignified fashion as though they were employees being dismissed, the Indians left the house. Santo and Isidro emerged from the forest where they had been hiding, speechless and sweating with terror. Then, in reaction against the strain of the day, Matter picked up his gun, aimed at a harmless tree-trunk and pressed the trigger.

There was neither bullet nor report; the weapon had jammed...

II

The days immediately after my return to the camp were among the worst of the whole expedition. Gradually the climate was wearing us down and each day a great lassitude sapped further at our ebbing strength.

It rained unceasingly, confining our world to the four walls of the hut. The only relief in the monotony was when the downpour slackened a little and allowed a rare visitor to join us. But even the visits were monotonous for their needs were always the same: they wanted to exchange feather ornaments for cloth, and the cloth was getting used up, bit by bit, under Ramon's mocking eye.

We sealed up the cases that contained our stuffed animals. We shot at the circles the rain made on the lagoon. We waged war against the vermin. We waited.

Matter, who was used to snow and great open spaces, struggled daily against the terrible effects of the tropical climate. His pluck never let him down.

Guébriant was calm, watchful and prudent as ever. His discomfort betrayed itself only by attacks of fever in the mornings. He never complained, but he was already weary when he rose from his bed. And I wrote letters that would never be sent, or noted our daily menu in the log-book: manioc and flaked oat soup; manioc and flaked oat soup; manioc and flaked oat soup.

To set the seal of our misery, we ran short of tobacco and had to make do with palm leaves. It was horrible, but the smoke kept us company and quelled to some extent the fury of the mosquitoes.

Vainly we hunted through our medicine chests for some drug to dispel our lethargy and stir us into life. But it was not drugs that restored our flagging spirits. It was the arrival of an Indian called Angush. He came early one morning. The rain had stopped the day before and under the sun's heat evaporation had begun. The forest was sweating profusely.

Angush, who had the reputation of being a fine hunter and warrior, sat down without ceremony on a wooden seat we had bought from his people. One of his three wives had come with him; she sat apart, near the filter, surprised, no doubt, that no music came out of it. (Nothing came out of it, least of all water).

Angush, impassively, explained the object of his visit. We were not, at first, impressed. The Jivaros, he said, had condemned a hostile witch-doctor to death. That was quite natural. Even more natural was the request that followed: for the loan of a gun. An ideal weapon for swift killing, no doubt, but why ask for ours when Angush himself possessed an old rifle, got by barter, which was still capable of firing a shot or two before it collapsed?

Angush said: "Give me your rifle and I will bring you back the magician's head and shrink it in front of you." There, in a few words, was the bargain he proposed. It electrified us. When he had left, with his wife and an old tin of food, we had a topic of conversation to last us the day.

It was an animated conversation. Guébriant refused point-blank to give up his Winchester in order that a man might be killed with it. I, on the other hand, proposed to offer my Mauser on the ground that either the Jivaros intended to take our arms, in which case no consideration would stop them, or else they genuinely wanted to punish a guilty magician and thus perform a rite we had no intention of suppressing.

Guébriant's reply was uncompromising. "A Jivaro's life is worth anyone else's," he said, repeatedly. He partly convinced us: enough, at any rate, for me to hang on to my Mauser. Angush came back next day with a different wife, but he went home empty-handed. Quite empty-handed, since there weren't even any tins of food to give him.

III

With the departure of Angush and the ending of the rains, we made up our minds to leave the Siguin and set up a camp lower down the river, towards the Morona. We intended to leave most of our cases of provisions and collect them on our way back to the north – a risky project but, having no extra canoes or canoeists, we had no alternative.

Ramon, with our help, was carefully classifying the last birds and mammals in the collection while awaiting the arrival of some gum, to be used for making waterproof bags, that Vitiap was to bring him.

But as we worked, a canoe grounded on our island and a curious figure climbed, without haste, the path to our hut. The man wore a peon's shirt and the standard pair of trousers got by barter. Under them, his emaciated frame was yellow with fever. His name was Francesco, and the story he told us was to change all our plans and lead us at last to the rite we had been longing to see: the ceremony of head-shrinking.

Francesco, the son of a Jivaro witch-doctor and a Cocama wife, was himself a magician. He knew a few words of Spanish and greeted us with "*Buenos dias*." We offered him a case to sit on but he preferred the bamboo floor and rejected the glass of sugared water we offered in favour of the jar of *yamanche* provided by Santo.

He had come, he told us, from Huachi, on the shore of the Pastaza, where he had a hut. How did he know we were camping here? He smiled; that fact was known as far away as the Cordillera of the Andes. White men who exchanged cloth for dead birds or spears.

His father, he told us, was called Yaouen, which means dog. Yaouen was a powerful man whose magic gift had cured a great many Indians and disseminated disease among hostile clans. His hut stood on the bank of the Rio Huasaga, on the borders of the Achual country, which from time to time was raided by the cruel Murato Indians. In those parts the huts are permanently fortified and war-traps laid on the paths.

Francesco's youth was spent among the alarms of war. His mother was of another race, a Cocama woman whom his father had won in exchange for some cure performed. Francesco learned from his father the invocations to the river Huasaga which are full of water spirits and cascades and singing fish:

"*Sungi, Sungi, Sungiri...* Spirit of the siren."

Francesco wanted to become a witch-doctor, and eventually he became one, but it was not from his father that he received his magic power. One night two warriors crept up to Yaouen's hut, to his bedside, after he had performed a cure and lay stupefied. Yaouen died, his throat cut by a spear, while Francesco, by his side, was spared.

The murderers came from the north, but they belonged to the same tribe; therefore Yaouen was not avenged. From that moment Francesco decided to kill the criminals himself. With a strength of will unparalleled among these Indians, who are slaves to tradition, he organized his life so as to get near them and be admitted among them and, when the day came, to act – and kill.

He went down the Huasaga as far as its junction with the Pastaza, continued southward alone in his canoe, and reached at last the vast mysterious Rimachi lagoon, home of the last remaining forest-dwelling Muratos, hitherto his deadliest enemies. He escaped their arrows and lived among them, learning their tongue and their incantations, and followed them when the group he now belonged to moved to the banks of the Pastaza to hunt tortoise. His aim was simple: to goad the Muratos as far as the murderers' hut and then, with their help, to exterminate its inhabitants.

Events happened differently. One day a canoe appeared near the huts set up by the hunters on a sandy island. A pale-skinned man was sailing it – no doubt a *mestizo* from

Iquitos seeking skins or gold. His arrival put all the Indians to flight and Francesco was left alone with the stranger. Two hours later Francesco exchanged his loincloth for a pair of trousers, which he was never to discard. Two months later he acquired a shirt and his new name. His patron cut his hair short and taught him a few words of Spanish. Later, Francesco became acquainted with the Indians from the Ukayali, who wore Peruvian uniform and practised shooting with rifles and automatic guns. But if he knew them, Francesco refused to live near them. He preferred to sleep in the canoe while his new friend camped with the soldiers. The rest of the time Francesco spent going up or down the big rivers on rafts laden with peccary skins. In this way he acquired cloth and thread and machetes and, more useful still, new skills. He learned how to catch fish with arrows, how to fix traps for certain animals, how to concoct poison for hunting from roots unknown to his tribe, but which the Indians living on the banks of the Tigre knew how to treat.

He learned to make practical use of the bones of monkeys, and how to distil new beverages. He was strong and tough and he became cunning, an adept at simulating joy and intoxication and friendliness. But his thirst for vengeance was not abated.

His patron died of fever during an excursion into the upper reaches of the Pastaza and Francesco's new-found liberty enabled him to go back to the huts of the Jivaro tribe which he had not visited for a long time. And there he met the men who had killed his father. The time for vengeance was at hand.

Yet Francesco did not kill the murderers. Francesco was a witch-doctor and the murderers appealed to him for help. He gave it, unable at last to break the strict force of custom which no resentment, no hatred, can overcome.

So, once again, Francesco had to bide his time and as he waited for an opportunity to avenge his father's blood he built himself a hut overlooking the Pastaza river. From there he travelled into the heart of the Jivaro forest, sailing alone in his canoe like the spirit of the river.

All this we learned from him that evening after a supper of sardines in oil, oatmeal soup and a cup of chocolate – none of which Francesco had tasted before. The mosquitoes flocked round the big eye of the electric lamp a few feet away from us and we smoked tobacco for the first time for weeks – tobacco in two long, carrot-shaped packets, tied up with flat lianas, which we had bought from Francesco.

But still we did not know what had brought him to us. Repeatedly we questioned him and at last he told us.

"*La guerra,*" he said.

He repeated the word, as we sat up and stared at him. War! But what sort of war? An Indian expedition or a solitary murder?

It was to be a witch-doctor, he said. A witch-doctor was to be killed. After the murder his head would be brought back by the murderers to a place appointed by the vengeful tribe and there it would be shrunk with full ceremonial rites. Francesco was seeking the hut to which the trophy would eventually be taken.

I looked at Guébriant; Matter looked at me. The same thought sprang to all our minds: here was our chance. We, too, were anxious to find it. Why not join forces with Francesco and seek it together, if he would guide us?

We broached the idea. We offered him cloth, a pair of trousers and, if the trip was successful, a rifle. The offer was too tempting to be refused and, by the light of the electric lamp, we at once measured off five yards of white cloth.

"We shall start at dawn," Francesco said, and lay down to sleep at the foot of my bed.

IV

Francesco immediately proved of great use to the expedition, a teacher as well as a guide. With him we learned how to find our way through difficult places and how to mark our route on palm tree trunks with great speed. Our journey through the maze of lagoons was not slowed down as it used to be. Now we inevitably grounded at a convenient spot. Even our canoeists could not conceal their admiration for Francesco's skill.

After several days' wandering along three rivers we reached a hut surrounded by the war-barrier, reminding us of the little fort on the Tunegrama. A steep path led to the low, narrow entry, where we were received without surprise by a dozen or so families living in an unbelievable state of destitution. There was no need to worry about possible firearms here; they had nothing.

Our presents – thread, mirrors, knives – aroused unanimous enthusiasm. The wives of one old warrior – he seemed to be the chief – began a frenzied dance. Hand in hand, leaping with both feet together and shouting words I could not understand, they surrounded us, retreating and then advancing close enough to touch us. For hours they danced around us by the light of wicks soaked in coconut milk and fanned flames, while we stood motionless.

Francesco, after a long silence, deigned to give us his opinion. "The women say you are their god," he said.

The next day began in this hut, as in all Jivaro dwellings, with the drinking of a hot infusion of awayusa round the fireside. Everything then went on quite normally until the early afternoon, when the Indians who had not gone hunting but were lounging on their beds began to show some agitation. They kept uttering short phrases to one another in which the word "coming" recurred frequently.

An hour later three Indians armed with spears entered the hut. Everybody stared but nobody got up. To my surprise I recognized three of the men from the Tunegrama hut.

I immediately told Francesco, who went up to them as soon as the customary ceremonial of welcome was over. With his *chicha* bowl in hand, he began a long discussion while we played with the children, learning some of their games, of which the favourite consisted of tying thread to the legs of big flies and watching them flutter round the hut. When supper-time came, I risked a few words in our guide's ear, but Francesco had drunk far too much. He only gazed at me vaguely, not quite recognizing me, and went on with his talk and drinking.

The days we spent waiting in that hut were among the strangest of the whole expedition. Forced to keep watch on Francesco, who was drinking bowl after bowl of *yamanche*, and thus condemned to follow suit, we ended by sharing the life of these Jivaros, sleeping on their platforms, daydreaming for long hours in the shade of the palm thatch. I did not pine for my anthropologist's outfit, nor Fred for his camera. Occasionally we remembered Ramon who had been left to guard the camp and was probably worrying, but we were not seriously perturbed about the possibility of being caught in a trap. Everything that was going on around us seemed completely reassuring.

V

One night the full moon was shining on the tree tops that surrounded the hut. Soft shimmering light spread as far as the eye could see, in harmony with the murmur of myriads of insects. For some strange reason the revelation of the vastness of the forest made our solitude unbearable. We were deeply moved, as though at the discovery of some hidden life.

A dance began. Women came out of the darkness of the hut, naked save for the white loin-cloth round their hips. Hand in hand, in a row, they faced the ring of supporting posts against which the men were leaning. At a signal given by one old woman, they leapt into the air together. Their feet struck the beaten earth in a rapid rhythm and as they danced they chanted: "*Pigue! Pigue!*" It means "Struck down."

Now to the right, now to the left, danced the long line of leaping figures. Unceasingly they uttered deep hoarse cries in which we could distinguish the ever-recurring word: "*Pigue! Pigue!*"

Hours passed; the night passed. The dancing women were allowed no respite. When one of them weakened her husband would rush forward and strike her roughly. "*Pigue! Pigue!*"

At dawn Francesco brought us the explanation. The enemy witch-doctor had been killed. Not far off, one day's journey by water, the shrinking of his head was going on. In a few days it would be brought to this hut with due ceremony.

In our delight we hardly listened to Francesco telling us the meaning of the dances. They were driving away the demon (*iguanchi*) from the hut...

ELEVEN : THE SHRINKING OF A HUMAN HEAD

I

The tribe had been wronged. A man had been killed and his death called for vengeance. At one time all the warriors of the hut would have sallied forth to war; now it was merely murder.

The raids of former days have been abandoned partly because of the dispersal of the Indian tribesmen and partly owing to the appalling mortality rate among children and young people which has resulted in a weakening of the race. Now, wisely, they go to the root of the matter: one man alone, the witch-doctor, is held guilty and struck down, while no blame attaches to the man who instigated the crime.

But death is not enough. The evil the witch-doctor has done must be forever sealed. His spirit must not be allowed to enter into another person and perpetuate the bad fortune. Therefore his head must be shrunk according to the traditional religious rites.

At this point we may well pause and reflect. We should try to forget the horror of the murder, of the deliberate hunt for a human head, of the blood that pours from the trophy. The concept of sacrifice, of an offering to propitiate the gods, is something unknown to us today; but we can at least avoid that violent repulsion which overcame the explorer Up de Graf. Confronted by similar scenes, which he describes with great emotion, he wrote: "I need hardly say that these Indians, like all mean-spirited creatures, are absolutely devoid of pity. Their moral sense is exactly comparable to that of a beast of prey." That was the opinion of an explorer whom I admire, who risked his life a score of times in bold adventures; but it should not be ours, since it is impossible for a white man to judge impartially a custom as apparently savage as head-hunting and head-shrinking. Its full religious significance escapes us and seems tainted with needless cruelty. But is this so for the Indian? He has two overpowering motives: the idea of vengeance and the wish to fulfil a sacrifice thought necessary to the community. There is no reason to suppose that the action of killing and beheading gives a sadistic pleasure to the warriors responsible for the execution. And even if it does, only a few would be involved. We must try to realize how every stage in the performance, from the first ambush to the preparation of the trophy, is governed by a sense of duty. Then we can more readily detach the rites and their significance from the fantastic setting. And from amid the songs and dances and revelry, the essential spirit of the Jivaro Indians, with all its intensity and precision, will be revealed.

We did not see the full ceremony and all its attendant acts at once, for the Jivaros keep armed guard over these highly secret practices. In this chapter I have combined two experiences; the first, which follows the chronological course of events, took place in the setting I describe. A few days later the Indians consented to repeat their ceremonies faithfully on the head of a monkey. Fred Matter managed to take films, and Jean de Guébriant photographs, which provide unique and admirable evidence of the custom.

The second experience confirmed the information thus obtained. It occurred three months later, when I was exploring by myself in the territory of the Huambiza Indians, near the Rio Santiago. On this occasion I witnessed the final rites of head-shrinking and the triumphal reception of the trophy. The victim was an Indian of the Makas tribe. A photograph shows an old chief holding this head. I have thus combined my notes to show as clearly as possible the procedure of these magic and religious rites.

II

In the hut, the members of the threatened *jivaria* prepared their defences as they had prepared them in the days of full-scale armed raids. They posted sentries at the doors of the stockade, prepared quantities of masticated manioc in case of siege, mended their weapons and made invocations before the bed of the man who had been slain.

But outside, in the darkness of the forest, the two Indians selected for the murder kept watch upon the enemy hut. They did not stand motionless in static ambush, but cunningly took advantage of trees and shrubs and the changing face of nature from dawn to dusk. When night began to fall they drew near the river that ran by the hut. Gun and spear in hand, they waited for their victim, as he waited for them. Songs and shouts reached them clearly, reminded them that their enemy must inevitably be panic-stricken, and this strengthened their self-confidence. They forgot their meagre rations and the *yamanche*, diluted with water, that goes sourer every day; they even forgot the hateful persecution of mosquitoes and venomous ants. The killing would take place soon now.

One evening, when the witch-doctor was making for the riverside to he with one of his wives, a wooden spear struck him in the throat. Without a cry he collapsed at the murderers' feet; his wife, too, fell dead.

In silence the killers bent over him and began to sever the head from the body. A long knife, acquired by barter, speeded up the work. In a few moments the trophy, still warm and bleeding, hung over the murderers' shoulders as they ran swiftly homewards. They hurried, although no one pursued them. The spears, gleaming with blood, were abandoned in a dense thicket; henceforth they were accursed and none would dare touch them.

Travelling with the utmost speed on foot and, when the river became navigable, by canoe, the men reached the place allotted for the ceremony of shrinking the head.

It was a good place. A clearing had been made amid the dense vegetation that crowded right down to the bank. The prow of a canoe had been pulled up on to the muddy shore. The ground had been trampled into hardness and covered with ferns and broad leaves. A slender tree-trunk was laid beside three smouldering logs.

As soon as they landed, the killers were met by the headman of the community, with two men and two women bringing food. They had been expected for many days; when they appeared everyone gathered round them, but nobody touched them. Amid suppressed excitement the head was laid down on a leaf; the ceremony of shrinking was about to begin.

First the scalp was removed. With sharp pins of black *chonta* wood the killers carefully slit the skin below the ear and made an opening down to the base of the neck. This gave them a hold on the skin, enabling them to pull it upwards towards the top of the skull; the process was as rapid and simple as skinning a rabbit. Nose, ears and eyes were the only obstacles, but the wooden pins served to cut the cartilages and gouge out the eyes from their sockets.

Two Jivaros together flayed the head and the bloody scalp was held up on a spear while the bones of face and skull were thrown into the river.

The headman, guardian of tradition, immediately fetched water. Dipping his vessel into the stream, he said: "I take the water of the boa."

The boa is essentially a beneficient animal and this appeal to its powers reveals the religious significance of the head-shrinking. These Indians are not merely concerned with preserving a war-trophy which shall bear witness of their valour. During the ceremonies, and by the mere fact of performing certain rites, they deprive the sorcerer of his baneful force. They believe that by reducing the size of the head – the seat of the spirit – by mummifying it, by sealing its lips, they can imprison its supernatural power. Thus they put the final seal on their enemy's death.

The water began to boil. Seizing the head, the chief called on the two murderers to lay their right hands on his hand. Thrice he threw the scalp into the vessel and pulled it out again before finally leaving it in to boil.

"I dip the head in the boa's water," he chanted.

"He is boiling the head," answered the two assistants.

For 15 or 20 minutes the Indians, in silence, watched the water bubbling, then, at a sign from the old man, they took the vessel off the fire. With a stick they fished out the scalp, now softened and purified, and hung it up on the spear

This completed the day's work. The participants sat on the ground to take their meal of small fish cooked in a wrapping of leaves, with manioc. Night fell suddenly. A tiny flame that defied that darkness kept watch alone, while the Indians, their loin-cloths wrapped about them, lay side by side, speaking to each other in low voices. At dawn on the second day we witnessed in silence the "rite of tobacco". The headman chewed tobacco leaves and then spat them into a shallow calabash. With his fingers he crushed and rubbed them to extract a thick liquid. Raising the vessel, he sucked it into his mouth and went up

to the murderers and the other participants. Each in turn bent back his head and received up their nostrils a dose of tobacco juice, spat with considerable force. The rite was repeated four times; its object was to protect the participants against the evil power still lurking in the trophy.

The two warriors now traced the outline of a skeleton with black paint on their bodies. A broad curved band at the top of the spine gave a strange shape to his shoulder blades. Between this and the waist were ten stripes, five on the chest and five on the back. Three stripes ran down each arm as far as the wrist. On the legs, between knee and ankle, were five stripes and an anklet. The face was simply indicated by one black gash prolonging the mouth into the middle of the cheeks. Now they confronted death as dead men themselves, having passed from the human world to the spirit world.

They set to work.

The trophy was taken off the spear and the hair bound with lianas. Then, with *chonta* wood pins, the headman pierced eyelet holes at the base of the neck. Through these he passed a thread on which he hung a ring of flexible wood. The head was thus transformed into a sort of pocket. The mouth was sewn up in the same way, by darts passed through the lips from below and surrounded with thread.

The participants sang: "*Ao apainaue.* He is sewing."

This was one of the most important rites, which henceforward condemned the

hostile sorcerer to silence. The eyelids were likewise pierced and sewn up. Now the process of drying by sand could begin.

The sand was being heated in a round, hollow plate. Nearby, a smooth stone lay exposed to the fire. The headman, followed by the two murderers, scooped up sand in an oblong calabash and poured it into the head. Then, shaking the head to and fro, they drove the sand in deep so that the heated particles might act upon the remotest parts of the scalp.

Fresh sand was constantly poured in. The flat stone, held by means of a folded leaf, was used on the outside skin. Through the dilated pores the flesh lost its fat and dried up. Sand and stone gradually transformed it into a sort of leather which grew harder every minute.

"*Wi yeyakim chumbiale.* I am pouring sand," the Indians repeated constantly, till night fell. A short pause allowed them to swallow the boiled fish the women had brought from the hut. When the trophy was once more held up on the tip of the spear it was already shrivelled and tanned and had almost acquired its final form.

The next process was, technically, a remarkable achievement. The ring binding the neck opening was tightened considerably and the head, firmly held in by the hair and the sheath of lianas, was massaged by the Indians. They pressed on the skin with thumbs dipped in ashes; they hollowed out the cheeks, shaped the nose, even gave the ears their original shape. Two days of this treatment, together with the continuous pouring of hot sand into the inside, produced the trophy.

Two-thirds smaller than a normal head, slightly narrower in proportion, with its lips protruding and maintained in that position by three darts, and the hair on face and head marvelously preserved: such was the Indian *tsantsa*.

On the evening of the third day the head was hung up on the spear and around it the dance called *Kongo-pi* was performed for a few minutes. Hand in hand the two warriors and the headman moved round it chanting slowly:

"*Kongo-Kongo-pi,*
Tawao-Tawao."

They were imitating the cries of forest animals in a supreme invocation to those who might have given refuge to the dead man's spirit.

As a precaution the scalp was taken down again, covered completely with leaves, and tightly bound up. It was to remain hidden from all eyes till the final purifications. Then the two participants got into their canoe, and while the last of night enfolded the sleeping camp they sped towards the hut to announce the imminent arrival of the trophy.

III

On a subsequent occasion I was to witness again the solemn reception of a shrunken head, but I never expect to experience the same strong emotion as in that hut on the Upper Siguin.

The war-drum sounded incessantly; visitors brought the good news to allied dwellings. Crowds flocked from all the nearby *jivaria*. Canoes landed lower down with loads of men, women and children. The stir and bustle transformed this wild corner of the forest.

During our absence at the shrinking some of the women had made a great number of earthenware vessels of various sizes to hold fermented liquor; others went to fetch manioc from the plantations and brought back a huge quantity of roots; others again sought the ripe fruit of the *chontaruru*. When everything was collected the grand session of mastication began. It was still going on as the final preparations were rapidly concluded under the watchful eyes of the old women, who never stopped singing.

The hunters brought back monkeys for the traditional *nassama* soup. Children went off to cut rushes and make them into flutes. The strongest men felled small trees, split the trunks into long logs and carried them near the fires. Plaited cotton wicks were soaked in rubber to light up the house for the night's dancing. New arrivals constantly swelled the crowd of friends and allies; provisional huts had to be erected for them, built of palms and plantain leaves and bamboos. Decidedly, this was to be a splendid feast of welcome!

Day broke, and the shouts and songs which had been going on all night gradually subsided. The old women began to deck themselves out with belts adorned with insects' wings, animals' teeth and seeds. We rose from the platforms on which we had been trying to sleep and looked out at the mist over the river. It was cold.

Suddenly a canoe appeared. At first it was a dark mass gliding through the fog; then, as it came nearer, we could make out, standing upright, the murderers and the headman. Two Indians who had met them during the night held the paddles.

The news of their arrival sent everybody rushing about, not in disorderly fashion, but in a way that proved how familiar, how carefully observed, were the various rites of the ceremony. Each group had its allotted place: the warriors near the river, by stools they had carried down; singing women under the eaves of the palm leaf roof, in a single row, turned to face the newcomers. The others, under or over age, stood apart.

The boat grounded. One of the oarsmen moored it to a tree stump and steadied it with his foot. One murderer got out first; he carried the *tsantsa* hung round his neck. The second murderer and the headman jumped out in their turn. Their faces bore visible marks of the deepest exhaustion, as befitted men who had spent a long time communing with spirits and had fulfilled the sacred rites.

The murderer in charge of the head sat down on the stool provided for him. Round him the men gathered in silence while the choir of women broke into a slow, wailing chant.

A procession was formed. In front marched the three heroes of the celebration, the headman between the two murderers, with his arms round their shoulders. Behind them came all the Indians, armed. As the procession entered the hut, the singing grew more passionate. When the head was hung beside its owner's bed there was a yell of joy: "Struck down! Struck down!"

Amid general rejoicing, those who had taken part in the shrinking were led by the chief to the stools specially set out for them. He took them by the shoulders and helped them to sit down, saying: "Those who have fasted shall crush the head."

At this point I confess myself mystified. I could not fathom the significance of this ritual gesture. Much of the ceremonial during this feast of welcome retains its mystery.

I found it difficult to be the perfect witness amid the excitement that, all around us, was mounting continuously to an alarming degree. But it was obvious that the Indians were undertaking some further magical measure of protection. Four times in succession, tobacco juice was spat into the nostrils of the four men and the choir of women accompanied the rite with the chant: "Drink in the tobacco."

After this, for the rest of the day, everyone could do as he pleased. The women took off their belts and bracelets and returned to their mastication. The men, in small groups, went down to the river to bathe or lay on the platforms and began interminable conversations. Jars of fermented *yamanche* were handed round. Shouts and even threats began to be heard. A sour smell pervaded the hut.

At sunset the men took out of their fibre wallets their ear-ornaments, red and black head-dresses, bamboo tubes holding paint for their faces. All got ready for the dances.

The first dance, the *Kongo-pi*, was performed by the headman and the murderers. The spear, thrust point downwards into the earth, upheld the trophy. When the opening words had been uttered the dancers began to move round it. Later all the guests joined in to a much faster rhythm, interspersed with shouts and animal-like howls, which lasted till the middle of the night.

After a light meal, everyone foregathered for the *Iiste* dance. All the fires were fanned and the fantastic shadows moving on the palm-leaf roof were duplicated by shadows huddled in close ranks on the ground.

The *Iiste* dance was a terrifying, and at the same time a monotonous, spectacle: a series of endless paroxysms. Hand in hand in a single line the women rushed forwards with a howl: "*Iiste! Iiste!* See! See!"

Behind them the men urged them on, or even struck them to quicken their pace. They ran for hours, without a pause, from end to end of the hut. While they ran forwards the chorus shouted, "*Iiste!*" When they ran back the whole assembly imitated the barking of the wild dog. Everyone was carried away by the din and each tried to outdo the rest. Once more I clearly felt that secret anguish to which these songs and dances give rise. These were no orgies. There was nothing here but fear, a carefully regulated fear. The spirits could not fail to recognize it.

A chilly dawn lit up the last spasmodic signs of life among the Indians. Most of them were sprawling on the ground or on their beds. It was time now for the murderers to rise. They had taken no part in the excitement.

They had before them a day of fasting and hard work. They had to prepare the rite of *wambo*, the purification of the trophy.

Two jars were brought, specially made jars that had never been used. One was to hold the *yamanche* of the three officiants, the other the *yamanche* to be offered to the *tsantsa*. But the fermented liquor must not be allowed to touch a vessel shapen by unclean hands; the murderers, therefore, prepared frames of light wood, finely trellised, and placed them at the bottom of the two vessels. On each of these they laid six plantain leaves, so arranged as to take the shape of the jar and hold the liquid.

All their actions were directed by the headman, to whom fell the task of pouring into each jar the necessary quantity of *yamanche*. Then, with a sort of spoon, he had carved himself, he stirred it lightly. A woman brought him two ripe, purple-skinned *agua* fruit (*saccoglottis guianensis*) which he seized and slit in four places, representing the four points of the compass. The four quarters were then laid between the plantain leaves and the sides of the jar. Thus the ritual food was prepared and protected.

We were the only spectators of these strange rites. The Indians, who had drunk far too much *yamanche*, were more interested in quarrelling with one another outside and in showing off their strength.

When darkness returned the dances began again, accompanied by even wilder shouts. Sleep was out of the question, which was just as well, for some drunken Indians came up to threaten us where we lay. Even Francesco, as excited as anyone, had bartered his trousers for a new loin-cloth. His schemes for revenge were apparently quite forgotten.

Next morning brought calm. The Indians' faces wore serious looks again. Now we witnessed the rite of purification.

A few steps away from the hut a broad shield, the *tandara*, was laid on the ground, handle upward. On it were placed the two vessels containing the ritual food and the black belt that one of the murderers was to wear.

On one side stood the chorus of women, their lower lips pierced by a dart, the arrow of bad luck, henceforward harmless. Opposite were the three officiants and a jar filled with water. The rite opened with the offering of *yamanche* to the *tsantsa*, now revealed without its covering of lianas. The liquid that touched its lips was promptly thrown away. The headman drank a mouthful from the vessel allocated to him; the murderers did likewise. Then the sacred liquid was thrown away in its turn.

The songs began. The head was held up over the big jar and its hair dipped under water and held there. The headman dried it by rubbing it repeatedly against his stomach.

A chorus of yells accompanied the ceremony. The din was increased by the clashing of wooden boards. Surely no evil spirits would dare venture into the neighbourhood! The wretched trophy was now undoubtedly segregated, vanquished for ever by its adversaries. Now it could be brought back in triumph, unveiled, into the hut.

All the men drew up in a line, one behind the other, led by the first murderer with the head hanging round his neck. Behind him came his companion, then the headman, the guest chiefs, the whole crowd.

"*Hum! Hum!*" cried the Indians, stamping on the ground.

"*Yakta!*" and they moved forward a few yards.

"*Hum! Hum! Yakta!*"

Thus the procession advanced towards the hut to which the chorus of women preceded it. When they came beneath the roof there was a general stampede. Guns were fired, spears were tossed wildly into the air. For the first time the head, brandished in a man's fist, led the warriors' dance. When the excitement died down the trophy was offered to the sun.

First it was fixed to a spear, according to the customary ritual: the first knot was tied by the headman, the others by the murderers. Thus secured, the head was lifted in the direction of the rising sun and then towards the west, while the women chanted: "*Etsa iista. See the sun.*"

The rejoicings continued with increased intensity for the guests although the sacrificers still had a day's fasting to observe. They merely pretended to drink *yamanche* while all around them the revelry was organized: literally organized, for here even drunkenness is meticulously regulated. The first to drink were the warriors, those who have already killed, who have won their spurs. Eight of them went up to the eight women who waited for them in the centre of the hut, holding vessels overflowing with the fermented liquor. A cry rang out and the men grabbed their cups and drank without taking breath.

Then a remarkable incident took place. Fred, who liked to take pictures of every conceivable subject, went up to the group of drinkers. Kuhi, who was among them, caught him by the hand and led him in front of the women.

"Have you ever killed?" Kuhi asked.

Fred did not answer, but nonetheless a vessel was handed to him and he drank, while a sudden hush fell over the crowd.

Then the revels began. With painted faces, ears pierced with heavy ornaments, necklaces dangling on their chests, men and women rushed wildly through the dwelling. Night increased their frenzy. Shrill cries rang out incessantly. Those who dropped out of the dance and sank down on the beaten earth, leaning against the walls, still kept up the chorus: "In my father's house let us dance. *Tutor! Tutor!*"

"Let the head dance! *Tuyung! Tuyung!*"

The dances of the chiefs and that of the murderers were riotously acclaimed: there was promise of gross delights in the dance of the women. These wretched creatures had not a moment's respite from serving drinks, dancing and submitting to their husbands' lust, none of which occupations seemed to afford them any pleasure. Only the virgins were granted any consideration, and if one of them occasionally ventured into the forest with a young warrior, she got something better than a beating there. Gradually the grown men began to quarrel and threaten one another and then, with a merciful hiccup, subsided. The murderers went about politely offering *yamanche* to the guests, holding the vessel at lip-height and saying: "*Amue!* You!"

Next morning when I woke I saw in the hut, strewn with sleeping bodies, a strange piece of apparatus, standing over 9 feet high and shaped like a cross. On its left arm the head was hung by a thread. Its cheeks had been daubed with magical red paint (*piako*) and its lips freed from the wooden pins that secured them.

I was able to witness the insertion of the mouth ornament, coarsely woven of white thread and passed through the three apertures. Five red threads, crosswise, exactly divided up the 15 inches of the ornament.

It has been said that the Jivaros were once acquainted with Inca culture, and that this ornament is closely related to the *kipu*, or counting frame, of the Peruvian Indians. Nothing justifies this supposition, particularly if one remembers that the Jivaros can only count up to three. They had no need to retain a highly complicated system of knots. Far more plausible is the theory that these threads, which are obviously designed to keep the enemy's mouth closed, had become ornaments now that he was rendered powerless. The cross bands indicated the number of victims of the victorious warriors.

After the ceremony, the headman and the murderers were supplied with *awayusa*. Thus they returned to normal life. Having swilled out their mouths with the hot infusion they drank a mouthful. Then they were ready to face solid food, boiled meat and palmetto hearts and manioc roots and the big piece of rock salt against which these eatables are rubbed. This was their first meal and they ate it with an appetite that can be imagined.

The best *yamanche*, made with fruits, was served to the three men – the sign for the rejoicings to start afresh. The murderers bathed in the river for the first time, rubbed the traced skeleton from their bodies, put on new loincloths, painted their faces and fixed feather ornaments in their hair. Purified, restored on equal terms to their kindred, they were welcomed with a frantic joy that abated only when the two men had set on the arm or breast of all present the black sign of the head-shrinking.

The others went on rejoicing as before, drinking, singing, dancing – what the old-fashioned explorers called "orgies". Then, to end up with, everyone flocked to the river to bathe, and the women were plastered with mud and ducked and beaten, all to the great delight of their husbands.

PART THREE : RETURNING

ONE : THE PARTING OF THE WAYS

I

Our camp rang with the noise of the hammers. A score of cases were lined up under a shelter, each bearing a number. One contained birds, another mammals, a third pottery. The larger objects, a war-drum, a seat, some blow-guns, and the bigger animals such as crocodiles, would travel uncovered save for a protective wrapping of plaited palms. The looms were wrapped in pieces of rubberized canvas specially prepared by Ramon. All that remained was to share out the provisions and medical stores.

Events were forcing us to separate. Guébriant, since the last day of the head-shrinking festivities, had been suffering from renewed attacks of fever. He was seriously ill and on the first night back in camp his temperature had risen steeply. Heavy doses of quinine had failed to bring it down. The injections provided by a chemist in Guayaquil had proved equally useless and I wondered why we bothered to keep the 150 phials, carefully set out in their cotton-wool cells. Jean and Matter, who had used up his 10,000 feet of film, were to go back the way we came. They had to. In this way Jean's life might be saved and the best results of the expedition and its documents would reach safety by the most direct route.

I was in no hurry to return. As long as my health would stand the appalling climate, I wanted to remain. The attraction of the region grew on me every day. The forest fascinated me – so vast that one could walk for 40 days and yet find it unchanged; so dense that its lianas intertwined from end to end unbroken; so rich that each of its myriad dead leaves concealed some surprise.

Ramon was to stay with me for a few days longer; we planned to work along a river in the north that I was anxious to explore.

Jean, sweating and shivering for hours on end, did not seem afraid of the long journey by canoe. He lay stretched out on his bed and lifted his mosquito net to watch us distributing the tins of food which were too heavy to take. The neighbouring huts sent emissaries to share in the bounty. They emerged from the forest in silence, their faces painted, their heads covered with feathers. The first-comers, at our suggestion, pulled out all the nails they could find to make harpoon-heads and fish-hooks. Those who followed sat down quietly on the bamboo floor and waited for the distribution to begin. They lined up, side by side, and we handed out thread and mirrors and needles. To some, with whom we had hunted and explored the forest, we gave knives and cloth. Nobody was jealous; nobody thanked us. Their faces remained grave and still, some bearing a streak of cruelty; we felt slightly embarrassed. One Indian did not even hold out his hand when I paused before him – there was so much dignity in his attitude that I hesitated to give him his share like a man intimidated in the act of tipping by the nobility of the waiter.

On an October morning, we hauled down the faded flag that had flown from the pole above our hut. Five canoes that Ramon had collected from the Chimikae Indians were already loaded with our cases and bags and were moored to the shore of our island. Our camp, denuded of all our tools and utensils, had a devastated appearance. The last waterproof bag, containing Guébriant's camp bed, blankets and mosquito net, was taken on board. Over the stretch of land we had cleared so laboriously, and where we had lived for the last few months, the forest was already growing. In a short time little trace would be left of our transient stay.

At the prow of one of the leading canoes a man hooted in his tortoise-shell, just as ocean liners hoot when they sheer off from the quayside. The journey began.

II

Rain was what we dreaded above all else and rain was coming. Already, huge drops made rings in the lagoon. We halted by a bank and hastily prepared a canopy of plaited palm under which Jean could lie. The air was sultry, but luckily the current was strong, and in a few minutes we had reached the Rio Siguin, running through the forest like a shady path. Two hours later we came to the Pastaza.

Big fish were leaping amid the eddies that marked the junction of the rivers. We harpooned a few before attempting to cross, so as to have something to cook once we reached the opposite bank. But to get there we had to push hard on our paddles and struggle against whirlpools. Our eyes and thoughts were fixed on the leading canoes as they launched out into the Pastaza, for they contained our collections. They managed well, keeping their bows pointed upstream in spite of a fierce drift. Ten minutes later they grounded on the further side, more than half a mile lower down. Our turn came; and our canoe, paddled by four men, took the impact of a mass of yellow water that covered us with spray. The trees wavered as though they were capsizing and then, in the huge rectangle of sky and river, we found ourselves puffing hard, moving crabwise towards the opposite bank. The effort made us sweat and we reeled with dizziness as we set foot on the shore.

That three-day journey upstream was among the most unpleasant of our expedition. The rain fell incessantly, close and heavy and monotonous. The river swelled hourly so that we were forced to hug the bank or else seek a less violent current on the further side. As we battled across the river we were carried downstream on the flood, losing in a few seconds what we had toiled more than an hour to gain. The Indians, untiring, had cut long poles, or *tanganas*, to punt with and constantly sought out the shallows, but there was no respite.

We all felt the need for haste. We wanted to reach Chambira where Jean could get some rest. Ramon, worried by Jean's high temperature, was hopelessly despondent. Guébriant, he said, was done for. His prophecies cheered me somewhat. Ramon was invariably wrong. When he foretold rain the sun would shine for 12 hours; when he predicted a drought we were drenched with rain and storm.

After 60 hours of almost ceaseless toil under a terrific downpour our five canoes reached a point opposite Chambira and our last crossing began. Huge tree trunks, sailing downstream at nearly 20 miles an hour and colliding with each other in the swirling current, imperilled the crossing and night was falling before we dug our poles into the sandy lagoon near the steep cliff. During the whole journey Jean had not once complained although he was drenched with sweat and water, tormented by mosquitoes and aching and feverish three hours out of every five. Fred, the Indians and I were full of admiration for him. Ramon merely said: "I told you so."

III

We began our stay at Chambira by hunting peccary; more exactly by hunting a peccary kept in semi-captivity by an Indian family. We wanted to lay in a store of its meat but to catch it we had to spend the whole day patiently stalking and chasing it. One of our guns, after four fruitless shots, gave up and exploded in the huntsman's face. The Indian family's manioc plantation was ruined by the headlong career of this curious domestic pig. But what a feast it provided when al last we caught and killed it – not to mention a fine store of dripping, *manteca*, which we collected and stored in an empty petrol tin.

Our food store was also replenished by fruit and animals given by the handful of Indians who live in this remote spot in exchange for the last remnants of our cloth and the tools we no longer needed. The food was invaluable. Guébriant and Matter would have to face a month's journey upstream without much chance of hunting or even fishing. The rainy season had begun, which meant that the rivers would be cloudy and the explorers compelled to live almost entirely in their boats.

Before I sent them on their way we engaged a new team of canoeists. They were all sturdy fellows, taciturn and brave. Most were venturing northward for the first time and, despite the magical paintings on their faces, they showed a somewhat apprehensive curiosity at the thought of travelling in the territory of other tribes. Their names were mostly Awasa and Kurioha, so that I got confused in my accounts when they came, one morning, to receive part of their wages: ten yards of cloth and a pair of trousers each. The distribution took place in semidarkness, under a roof of palm-leaves. I could barely distinguish one from another for their faces were equally dark and bedizened and their gestures identical. When the payment had been made they assembled in a corner to try on the trousers under their loin-cloths. They were all delighted and the whole gang set off in the pouring rain with their legs enclosed in their newly-won trophies.

At last came our final evening together. Dusk was short. At six o'clock the shrill whistle of insects pierced the monotonous sound of the rain. Under the palm-leaf shelter that served as our kitchen the fire suddenly flared up redly. In the hut where we were camping our beds stood round the hurricane lamp into which flies and mosquitoes kept falling. We were smoking our pipes peacefully, our quick meal eaten. Guébriant lay on his bed, Fred wrote on his knee, I day-dreamed with my chin in my hands. I thought: our little group has been swayed by the same emotions, we have pooled our suggestions and discoveries, we have even thought in common.

Yet tonight something had changed. The rustle of the forest close at hand, the moist heat, the reflex actions provoked by the incessant stinging of the anopheles, all the details of our recent evenings were reproduced and yet we were affected differently. My friends were thinking about their next day's journey; I was to go in quest of other scenes. The cases remaining in the hut were mine and mine alone. The time of parting was at hand.

I shook myself and stood up. Why dwell on it? We could not allow ourselves the luxury of feeling blue. It was better to go to sleep.

"Good night, all," I said and to their murmured replies I turned in and instantly fell asleep.

IV

The seventh day of rain. In the early morning mist Guébriant and Matter folded the camp beds and packed them in their waterproof covers. With their boots on their feet and their revolvers on their belts they breakfasted with me for the last time. Then we all went down to the shore.

The river was in full spate. The canoes were tugging at their liana moorings. We shook hands. A few minutes later the five canoes pushed off. The current was so strong against them that three hours later the flotilla had not yet passed the first bend. I could still see it, close to the bank.

Ramon did not stop playing the gramophone.

V

That same evening Fred Matter wrote in his diary: "Said goodbye to Bertrand. About 4.45 stopped on a wide stretch of shore. Mosquitoes. Still raining. At 9 p.m. the chief oarsman woke me up. The river was in spate. It had risen to within ten feet of the camp which the canoeists had set up a short time ago 30 yards from the water. I could see only one boat. Where were the rest? Lower down, he said. The men had moored them up. Thank Heaven!"

Next day, after a night of alarms:

"The Pastaza seems somewhat lower but the current is still as strong. At one o'clock, stopped on a shore. We hadn't been there ten minutes when a sudden flood drove us off. We finished the oatmeal soup in the boats...

"Mosquitoes – clouds, sheets of them. The canoeists wanted to stop. We made them go on..."

Another day and the situation had grown worse:

"At 7 p.m. we set off from the corner of the forest where we had vainly tried to sleep, but the eddies carried off the canoes. It took over an hour to make up the 300 yards we had lost. It rained incessantly. Tree trunks sailing downstream at top speed held us up. The canoeists fixed up the camp.

"Midnight: look out – water within two yards of the camp. We carried our beds higher up. Jean had a fresh attack of fever. Three a.m.: water still rising. A fresh removal. Five a.m.: I awoke to find myself flooded. We barely had time to collect our floating possessions and get to the boat. Mosquitoes! Mosquitoes! How do the canoeists, who go half-naked, stand it? Personally I am sick of the forest, sick to the teeth. So is Jean."

My friends struggled upstream for more than 20 days. Twice they changed their entire crew, the only companion which stayed faithful being their little tame *coati*.

But at last they reached the outside world, to find well-deserved rest, and peace from the Amazon.

TWO : THE LONELY JOURNEYS

I

The next three months brought me a kaleidoscope of emotions and places. I sailed along many rivers, slept in the outposts of the Peruvian "empire", lived alone among the Huambiza Jivaros along the Santiago and the Potochi rivers. They were months of revulsion and contentment, of compassion and boredom, of friendliness and hostility. And all the time my strength slowly ebbed. The forest was taking its toil. Soon it would drive me home.

II

The day after Jean and Fred sailed away from Chambira, a big canoe, manned by four Jivaro Indians, arrived at the settlement and temporarily changed my plans. I had intended to go first to Puerto Soplin, a little miracle of civilization in the heart of the forest. Instead I went into the depths of poverty.

Of those four Indians, two were ravaged by *pian*. Their bodies were repulsive with the disease, their finger-tips bleeding. I plucked up courage to attend them, when they had got over their initial distrust of me, and they showed their gratitude by taking me to their hut, deep in the densest forest I have ever seen. This remote dwelling was pervaded by such terrible distress that my first impulse was to leave it immediately. Every member of the group was infected by *pian*, and they dragged out a hopeless existence within the narrow space the forest allowed them.

We stayed long enough for Ramon to stuff a monkey and a few birds, and for me to empty my box of presents and take a few notes. Three days after our arrival we took the same route back, as fast as we could travel.

III

Ten days later – only ten days – and, lo and behold! I us sitting with my elbows on a real table, in front of plates made of "real" china. Coffee steamed and shimmered in my cup. Beyond the fresh bread and butter, beyond the sugar-bowl and the coffee-pot, sat a young man in uniform, an officer.

This was Puerto Soplin, first Peruvian military station, advance bastion of the Inca Republic. The day before, we had watched a bare, treeless space appear like a mirage on the steep forest bank. As the current bore us nearer we made out three or four iron-roofed houses. It was a military encampment, one of those amazing spots amid the greenness of the map where Peruvian colonists have chosen to display their energy. Twenty men had landed there a year before, attacked the forest with their machetes, cleared and drained the land and built their huts. As none of the men had stood the terrible climate for more than a month, others had taken their place.

As I drank that memorable cup of coffee, with intense enjoyment, two gangs of soldiers marched off to work at the road-cutting. From the tall flagstaff floated the red, white and red standard.

The sub-lieutenant in charge of the post was full of consideration. He told me that his government had sent instructions about our expedition. I was to receive every sort of assistance, he promised me, and it proved true. Seated in an armchair opposite the little house, the *commandancia*, I could not help thinking about the days that had passed and the days that were to come. I heard songs, the sound of hammers, orders, bugle-calls. In the evenings I was even able to read military journals in which I recognized French names, or dilapidated magazines where all the improper pictures bore Parisian inscriptions. From his bed besides mine the sub-lieutenant explained to me his colonization schemes and was puzzled because he had never met a single Indian, a single Jivaro. He went on to talk about war and poison gas...

But in the night the tenuous veneer of civilization was torn off by the grim sounds of the vengeance of the forest. The stillness was broken by the cries of sufferers from malaria, shaken and terrified.

"We spend our time evacuating men and bringing in others. What a business!" grumbled the officer, as he got dressed beneath his mosquito-net.

This square of land on the edge of the river, still covered here and there by huge tree-trunks, provided many surprises. The greatest was a bit of pasture where the station's bull and two cows were grazing. The animals had travelled for nearly a month by raft to reach this prison in mid-forest! The bull died two days after my arrival, stung by some sort of viper.

"He was the sixth," said the sub-lieutenant.

The edge of the forest, like a green curtain of closely-woven trees and creepers, marks the frontier of civilization. Ten steps further in you have to cut your way with a machete; you are in Indian territory. The soldiers on guard realize it and never take their eyes off the dark mass. One memory must be imprinted on their minds as indelibly as their passwords: the Jivaro attack on the Morona station in which more than thirty soldiers were slaughtered and the wives of the N.C.O.'s carried off.

I began to understand the fear these men concealed behind a mask of energy. I began to feel it myself, now that I had grown re-accustomed to forgotten comforts like bread, filtered water and grilled meat. The bugle-calls had a tragic ring amid the loneliness.

I must think about starting out once more.

IV

While I was explaining my itinerary to the sub-lieutenant, tracing it on the map with one finger, there was a knock on the bamboo door.

"*Adelante.*" ("Come in.")

In the doorway stood an Indian. He was small and swarthy, fearfully thin and clad in trousers. The floor creaked under his broad feet.

"*Correo.*" ("The mail.")

That blessed single word! I could grow lyrical about it. The Indian was named Octavio. He had been baptized and belonged to the Dominican mission of Canelos. His worn face bore traces of his 18 days' journey by river to fulfil the inspiration of the missionaries and bring me my letters.

We offered him a drink. A little glass of *aguardiente* set him off talking. He had met Jean and Fred on the Upper Bobonaza. Really, fate is sometimes astonishing.

And here was the mail. Octavio pulled out of his pocket a big packet tied with string and sodden with water. With the lieutenant's permission I made for the riverside and, sitting on a tree trunk, tore open the first envelopes I had touched for months.

V

That evening after supper the little garrison gathered round a fire, where a huge tree-trunk and some branches were burning. The mosquitoes were so aggressive that you got used to breathing smoke. At about nine p.m. their number decreased considerably and it was possible to go indoors again.

Once more the sub-lieutenant and I looked at the map. The Pastaza flows in a straight line for about 120 miles till it meets the Marañon. Straight lines are straightforward, at any rate!

"One more day's journey up the Marañon in a canoe you will find the Barranca station where they will be expecting you," said the sub-lieutenant. "From there you can easily travel wherever you like among the southern regions. We can let you have the motor-launch to go down the Pastaza and four men to go with you."

"When can I start?" I asked.

"Tomorrow morning, if you like."

That same night the soldier in charge of the boat was smitten with malaria. Two days went by. Ramon, who was bound for the north, shipped his cases on to Octavio's canoe and I presented him with a large stock of provisions and a portable stove.

The third day, at dawn, the launch backfired loudly on the river. I said goodbye to the station commander, to Ramon, to the soldiers lined up on the edge of the cliff, and we set off, sailing down with the current towards other regions.

VI

The first day's sailing on the river, which grew continuously wider with enormous bends, was uneventful. That evening we camped out in a hut at the confluence of the Pastaza with a river called Manchari. I have seldom suffered so acutely from mosquitoes!

The second day we were off by four a.m. under drizzling rain. At noon we halted on a small island where quantities of quite tame birds were sheltering. In the evening we passed near the famous Rimanchi, or Rimachiuma, lagoon which the Indians of the district regard as the last refuge of the cruel Muratos. Apparently it is impossible to reach it – so at least thought the driver, a civilized native from the Rio Ukayali, who described to me the misdeeds of the Muratos. As I suggested trying to penetrate the vast marshland, the engine stopped! We had run out of petrol. So there we were, condemned to float downstream in the gathering darkness, in our heavy and unmanageable boat.

In spite of the coolness we were invaded by mosquitoes. In silence we ate some cold and gluey oatmeal soup and a piece of fish. As we each sat in our places, ready to jump into the water if anything went wrong, we spent the night looking at the sky and driving off the mosquitoes.

In the morning we saw on the left bank of the Pastaza a big, bare, ochre-coloured tree standing high above the line of the forest. It was a capirona. When they saw it the soldiers shouted: "Marañon! Marañon!"

It was so. A few minutes later we emerged into a sort of estuary a mile and a quarter wide – the confluence of the Pastaza and the Amazon.

I was deeply moved. There was the Amazon, rapid and majestic, mysterious and legendary. How could one fail to be impressed by that great mass of brown water, flowing like a solid block between the two walls of forest? The sight was not so very different from that of other rivers I had seen. But one name blocked out all other memories: a name familiar to zoologists, geologists and geographers as well as to poets: the Amazon!

THREE : THE DYING INDIAN

I

At Barranca, a garrison established on a cliff on the left bank of the Marañon, between the Pastaza and the Morona, I had plenty of time to plan out an expedition into the southern territories, where I expected to find the Aguarunas.

These Indians, who belong to the Jivaro tribe, live near the three tributaries of the right bank: the Potro, the Apaga and the Nieva. The Potro is downstream, three days' journey (it takes seven to sail up it again); the Nieva is three weeks' journey upstream; the Apaga not more than four days' journey upstream. The owner of the canoe which I chose for the journey travelled along the lower reaches of this river and described it as uninhabited as far as the junction of two rivers which he called Yanapaga and Yurapaga. Here, he said, lived two Aguaruna tribes which spread as far as the foothills of the Cordillera of the Andes.

The origin of the name Aguaruna seems to me a combination of the words *agua*, water in Spanish, and *runa*, man in Inca. "The men of the water." The Marquis de Wavrin holds that Aguaruna is an altered form of a Jivaro word *aguahum*; personally, I have never heard such a word spoken.

Such minutiae evidently did not worry my two canoeists. To them any creature with long hair and a loin-cloth was a *salvaje*, a savage or heathen. These two stout fellows, somewhat spineless when left to themselves, always reacted in front of me with pride and remarkable stupidity. They knew the role they had to play in any region with which the white man was unfamiliar so they served as intermediaries between the forest and its would-be conquerors: it was a sort of vocation with them, handed on from father to son.

Their speech was a hotch-potch of Spanish and Inca, native words and names of rivers, but they were excellent, patient oarsmen. Where such types settle near the passionist missions or military stations, like spiders at the centre of their web, they depopulate the neighbourhood, or real Indians shun them. The pure Indian, the proud Jivaro, loathes everything that savours of cross-breeding and compromise. The fact that he is willing to barter does not disprove this fact. In any case it is not uncommon for ten years of peaceful commercial relations to be cut short by a murder.

After ten days at Barranca I was in much better shape, thanks to normal food and the kind attention of the station commander. Then I started up the Marañon with the new canoe and my two men. As the river was rising, it took us five days to reach an island opposite the mouth of the Apaga. We got there after strenuous efforts, catching sight in the distance of the black waters of the swift Morona. On this island was a house, or rather a hut on stilts with bamboo outhouses, where I found evidence that Rafael Karsten had been there. A woman lived there and directed a squad of long-haired peons who, as I approached, hid in the plantation.

She was past her first youth, yellow or brown-skinned according to the time of day, and she wore a dress; she was the Mujer of Don Romolo Rojas. (The term implies a distinction between a Mujer and a Senora). She received me in her bamboo-floored hut with the rough kindliness of such creatures, who are permanently lost in the forest. Her husband was travelling along the rivers, seeking salt and skins. It was a pity, for he had a close, indeed a unique, acquaintance with these regions, where he had lived for 16 years.

"You'll meet him one of these days on his raft," she said to me naïvely. "You'll see, he has a beard."

II

Don Romolo Rojas did indeed have a beard, a vast fan-shaped beard. We had been sailing along the Apaga for three days when, coming round a bend in the river, we saw his raft.

Sitting inside my *pamakari*, my protective cage of palms, I caught sight of him and stood up in the prow of the canoe to call him.

"Senor Rojas, good-day!"

The only answer was an inhospitable grunt, but nevertheless the raft changed course and grounded on a beach. Our canoe drew up beside it, and we two men faced one another under a sun at its zenith, with the awkwardness that belongs to those who have spent long months in vast lonely spaces. Don Romolo looked at me for a while without speaking, then he held out his hand.

"Good-day," he said.

An hour later we were friends. This extraordinary adventure-seeker gave me all sorts of information about the Indians, the nearby hills where he had seen the entry to a subterranean passage, and the protective barriers set up by the Aguarunas.

"They are at war," he told me. "I was unable to go up further than the junction of the two Apagas. I don't advise you to. Come back with me."

As I refused, he wished me good luck and added: "I'd gladly come with you, but I'm going to Iquitos. I shall be there within a fortnight, maybe. I shall see my mother, *mi mama*, whom I haven't seen for over 20 years. Goodbye."

Before we parted Don Romolo gave me a useful hint for catching otters, which are numerous in these rivers. Then he got back on his raft, waved and moved off.

III

For the next six days I was conscious only of my Indian oarsmen, who took their rest beside me at our midday or evening halts. Our group of three men, sparing of speech and gesture, was the entire population of the river. Not a hut was to be seen, not a canoe lying deserted at the opening of a path. Gradually one's conception of the countryside, of a village, began to alter. Even Romolo's beard seemed a memory from another world.

Meanwhile I kept returning, as to a drug, to the letters, envelopes, and newspaper cuttings I had received at Soplin. I read them at night, protected by my mosquito-net. The element of bitterness or grief in each of them appeared more clearly at each reading, as though written in some invisible ink that revealed itself during my insomnia. How weary this page seemed! I tried to conquer the elementary weariness of the traveller and to sympathize with the weariness of the written page.

My Indians, under their palm-leaf roof, with their feet to the fire, were telling stories of the forest. That was happiness. The bull-frog, croaking its monotonous cry, which we didn't drive away, nor tried to silence, that was happiness. So was our solitude in the heart of the deserted forest.

Here sleep knows no good night, awakening no good morning. There are no wishes. Tomorrow at dawn the oarsmen would resume their task of cutting up the otter we killed this afternoon and which lay outspread on a bamboo frame. Life was without vain hope, because it was without regrets. Forward, and good hunting!

Late one afternoon we reached a hut on stilts overlooking the river, some ten or twenty yards from the bank. The path that led to it was overgrown with weeds. The house was empty. On the platform opposite we found plantains covered with clusters of *papayas*, those big, juicy, insipid fruit whose flesh you scoop out of the skin, and further on two oarsmen laid in a store while I hunted through the hut. There was nothing left except a half-broken jar. On the slightly raised hearth we made a fire; it was good to be able to prepare fish soup and rice without having to fight off the evening mosquitoes.

We moored the canoe securely and, when night fell, we lay down, all three side by side, on the bamboo floor, our feet towards the dying fire.

IV

How beautiful this river was, how different at every turn! It flashed forth surprises, or bore them along in its reflected heaven. Some travellers, I thought, are never happy unless they can bring in God. Every sight they see – the flight of fearless parrots, the meticulous life of a tribe in its huts – they adduce as proof of His presence. But my Indians and I existed in a state of such humility, such simplicity, that we felt the divine action without need of words. I had already attained that abnegation towards which the pious strive!

As for detaching oneself from the outside world to lose oneself in contemplation or mystic ecstasy, I realized how improbable and even ironic that would be, when we had

constantly to defend our soup from the flies, our necks from the mosquitoes and our slumbers from venomous ants.

V

Don Romolo had told me that when I had passed the forty-third bend of the river after our meeting place, I should come upon a Jivaro hut on the left bank. Beyond this point it was not safe to venture.

One morning, landing from our canoe, we found a path before us and followed it; and at the end we saw this hut. No human face was to be seen there, no dog was barking.

The silence made me cautious. My oarsmen, following in my footsteps, moved more slowly still, their restless eyes watchful. So, in Indian file, we reached the hut, which was surrounded by a bamboo wall, and boldly pushed open the door.

At first, in the darkness that succeeded the white day-light, I could make out nothing. The hut seemed to be empty but the sound of someone gasping for breath guided my steps. I went up to a platform and saw an Indian, completely naked, bent double. At his feet stood a woman, leaning backward in terror, staring at us with wide, open eyes. The sight of this terrified pair gave my men courage. I spoke a few words in Jivaro to him, and, astonished, he answered me in a faint voice. He must have considered my arrival a supernatural phenomenon and, to judge by his behaviour, not a sinister one, for he sat up, tied his loin-cloth around his waist and told the woman to blow on the embers of the fire.

The rest followed quite simply. My camp bed, my sleeping bag and the medicine-chest were carried up to the hut and, without fuss or argument, I intervened in the lives of these two creatures. The old man had to be attended to promptly, for he was terribly ill.

I could not explain what drew me to this fine old fellow who lay there at the point of death, panting, drooling over his hairless chest. He swallowed, without astonishment, the aspirin I gave him and some drops of an oxygen preparation. I covered him as best I could with my blanket, and hoped for the best.

In the evening, at sunset, he bathed in the river. At night the woman fanned him with big palm-leaves.

"Is she your wife ?" I asked.

"No, my son's wife," he said.

"Where is your son?"

"In a hut on the right-hand river [the Uanapaga], for they are at war over there."

The oarsman Juanito was preparing our meal in the hut.

"Have you got any manioc?" I asked.

"Oh no," replied the woman. She showed me a vessel half-full of *yamanche* so sour it would have disgusted the least fastidious. That was all they had to eat. Clearly, we had come just in time to save their lives.

Everyone did justice to Juanito's oatmeal soup and boiled fish, and the tea that followed. During the evening the old man seemed anxious to speak and I sat down beside him to listen to his strange story.

A long time before – a year maybe – he told me, fever had smitten the hut. Many families had been living there – all nine beds had been filled. The men had died as well as the children – even the strongest, those who sailed in their canoes up to the Santiago river to seek spearheads, and went hunting as far as the hills on the track of their quarry. The witch-doctor had been one of the first to die. One evening he had drunk his magic draught and gone deep into the forest to consult the spirits. He did not return. They had to bring back his bloodstained corpse one day, to perform the funeral rites. After that nobody put up any fight. Now he, the headman, and his daughter-in-law were the sole survivors. Raising the first finger of his left hand the sick man recited like a litany:

"*Vikia akae*

Chiki akae

Nuha akae..."

His four wives were dead! He added with a gentle ironical smile, "I am dead, too!"

The young woman did not contradict him, but gazed at me attentively. And I looked at her too, in silence. I watched her get up and go down to the river where she bathed, quietly, holding her breasts in her hands. In the evening she brought me the soup she had prepared and, later on, came to lie down noiselessly on the platform beside my camp bed.

Next day it was plain that the old man was recovering. I left him some aspirin and instructed Irraret, the young woman, how and when to use it. Then we set off once more.

A few hours later we reached a collection of some dozen huts made of leafy branches. Only a few were inhabited, by Indians of unprepossessing aspect. As soon as we arrived they gathered together and quickly let me know that I was an intruder. The man who spoke to me was young, the least unpleasant of the group; but he brought along with him a deformed, repulsive creature whose face was half eaten away, who had no nose, and whose cheeks were two red patches. This, they declared, was the work of a worm deposited at night by evil spirits. I thought that a course of treatment with some arsenical preparation would do him more good than the invocations of a witch-doctor; but I had no time to explain my point of view. I had to hurry to get back to the canoes where my two oarsmen were already waiting for me. I could hardly persuade them to start off up the river but I managed it at last. I hoped that my treatment of the sick man would ensure for us the gratitude, or at least the neutrality, of the Aguaruna.

A little further on we found a fine beach sweeping round in a huge semicircle, on which we drew up our canoes. It was a good place for camping: plenty of open space and not too many mosquitoes. Its only disadvantage was the number of water-snakes. They made bathing impossible.

We stayed in this blessed spot for ten days, shooting splendid birds of every colour, or fat red-billed water hens. We had only to raise our eyes to enjoy the wonderful display given by the *colondrinas* as they darted swiftly about and teased the squat parrots and the screaming parrakeets. Noisy monkeys flocked to within a few yards of our tents to stare at us. And it did not rain once. The sky was uniformly bright blue or starlit. Never, throughout the whole expedition, had I spent such wonderful moments – until the day when Juanito ran up to disturb my siesta by announcing that he caught sight, behind the rushes, of the Indian with the mangy face, and that, moreover, this Indian was armed with a rifle.

It was true. But this terrible creature was only the herald of various groups of Aguarunas who landed in canoe-loads of two or three families. Without delay, I began to hand out objects – thread and mirrors. Afterwards, all the men consented to be measured, and presented ornaments and loincloths which enriched my collection.

A little later I was able to go into one of the Yanapaga huts and collect some information there. I noticed particularly that the dwellings were closed in and well protected against attack. The beds, although they stood close to the bamboo wall, were each guarded by a raised screen about a foot high. In front of each, near the hearth, stood the *patachi*, consisting of a wooden bar supported by two small forked stakes, on which the sleeper's feet rest. The fires were kept up all night. It was cool, for the mountains were close at hand.

The oddest object I found during this visit was a musical instrument shaped something like a violin, hollowed out of a single block of light wood and covered with a lid of the same wood.

Two strings made of finely plaited fibre completed this instrument: the *tchaku*. A bow of equally primitive design drew from it a few musical notes. It served, no doubt, to accompany the reveries of Aguaruna poets.

But my oarsmen saw nothing poetic about the Aguarunas. They nagged at me ceaselessly with their complaints. Fearing the worst – I could not tell why – they wanted to get back to their own land. Probably they were right. At any rate I realized that I could persuade them to go on no further up the river, so back we went towards the Marañon.

FOUR : THE LAST EXPLORATION

I

I lay back in the canoe, overcome by a feeling of oppression that now never left me and watched the two Huambiza Indians punting me along the tumultuous waters of the Chinganasa river, one of the tributaries of the right bank of the Rio Santiago. It was the first time I had gone exploring with the Huambizas; it would also be the last. My health was going. My head was rarely free from a continual buzzing; the enthusiasm that once had borne me up was ebbing fast.

I reflected with some emotion on these two Indians as I watched their naked figures in the prow silhouetted against the landscape, bending rhythmically over their long poles.

I had had ample opportunity to study the Huambizas in two or three huts of the *jivaria* of the Katirpesa, the only one on the banks of the Santiago, not far from the small outpost of Cabo Reyes. They were akin to the Achuals and the Aguarunas, but more powerful, more warlike and considerably more polygamous. I witnessed the reception of a shrunken head. The ceremony was accompanied by festivities in which nearly sixty Indians took part, together with innumerable women and children, and I was able to fill a good many pages and measurement charts. But what chiefly struck me about them was that they seemed to hold me in deep contempt. They made me pay a high price in cloth or tools for any object I bought for my collection. But once the bargain was struck they encouraged me to depart as quickly as possible.

The canoe grounded. I wondered idly how the people of the Chinganasa would receive me but I was not greatly worried. I was past worrying.

I entered their hut, enclosed by its war-barrier, passing on the way a boy with a swollen belly caused by drinking too much fermented manioc. Inside it was no different from those I had already visited. Four supporting posts and about 30 stakes placed in oval formation made up the framework of the dwelling. Against the wall were the nine platforms and in front of each the *patachi* and the traditional hearth. But only two fires burned: the rest were dead.

On the high shelf, five yards wide, that stood in the middle of the hut, were earthenware vessels and huge jars that doubtless contained bones. Against one of the posts, slung through a great ring of lianas, were the hunting weapons, blow-guns and spears. Three stools were set round a vessel into which a certain amount of *yamanche* had been spat.

Only two families now lived there. The two husbands sat up when I came in and, without speaking a word, lay down again on their beds. A curious welcome!

The elder was called Yaouen, which seems to be a common name among the Jivaro people. His intelligent face was crowned by thick hair coiled like a turban, and he wore a large necklace. He seemed to enjoy a certain authority for he ordered a woman to fetch me a stool and the *masato* with which visitors are welcomed.

Yaouen, his companion Tie, who was drowsing on the neighbouring bed, and their wives and children formed a quiet little group that lived self-sufficiently in this corner of the forest. I looked hard, but could find nothing of extraneous origin save their women and the poison for their darts. From dawn to dusk they had less than 50 square yards to move about in, but apparently it was enough for them. The river, whose waters were unusually clear, provided them with fish, the forest was well stocked with game and their manioc plantation, their *chacra*, was far from exhausted. A few tobacco plants and plenty of cotton provided for their religious ceremonies and their clothing needs, and they had not far to go along the first path to find the lianas for concocting *natema*, and the seeds for face-paint and the leaves for dyes. Even the big stone which the women used for pottery-making stood in its place at one end of the shelf.

The witch-doctor, like a visiting priest, passed that way during the dry season. In his honour great quantities of magic drink would be prepared and for three or four nights his songs of healing and his invocations to the spirits would bring these people the comfort of a supernatural presence.

It was a carefree oasis, untroubled even by mosquitoes or vampires, and I should have been grateful, for it had taken me a long time to find. Instead I was bored. The dwelling was too lonely, the seven empty beds and the seven dead fires depressed my imagination. When, tired of watching the swiftly-flowing stream, I asked to be taken further into the interior, I was met by a refusal more categorical than the forest itself could have given me.

This, then, really was journey's end. My Huambiza guides had long since fled and I could not penetrate the forest alone. The two paths that started off towards the north stopped short after 50 yards in an inextricable tangle of lianas and shrubs, a dense growth of leaves shaped like spears and saucepans and fountains which sank a little under one's steps but would not yield.

Yaouen assured me that those who went off that way never came back. Yaouen was probably right.

I sighed and gave up the idea. I would stay here awhile. After all, Tie had a young daughter, not quite mature, but very sweet. Tie wanted to be friends with me. Tie was probably right.

II

From time to time I shaved because the insects took a liking to my beard. It was quite an effort but Tie's daughter was really very pretty. The whole family took part in the performance. Endsa, the youngest, went to fetch water. Yaouen held the mirror, often turning it round to watch himself laugh. The young girl laid her hand on my cheeks to make sure they were smooth.

That was as far as my efforts to be civilized went. The tinned food was finished and the empty tins were used to hold head-feathers. I shared the Jivaro menu: at dawn the infusion of *awayusa*; at midday, when we got the chance, boiled monkey-flesh and a few pieces of manioc, and at night fish smoked in a wrapping of leaves. Sometimes we enlivened our diet with *konguki*, a fruit shaped like big olives, peculiar to this region. I was told that, when treated in a certain way, the *konguki* yield an oil which makes the hair grow. We did not try it but we enjoyed eating them.

The children grew used to me and played freely in my presence. They danced, they threw branches or short spears made for them by their fathers, but nothing delighted them as much as chasing flies. There were some tiny flies, almost invisible, whose sting causes painful itching; and there were big buzzing ones that hovered over the fermenting *yamanche*. These the children caught easily; they tied long threads to their legs and then let them loose in the hut. Amid shouts of excitement the flies fluttered here and there, held on the leash by their captors; the one that stayed longest in the air had won. I found the game fascinating and I made up my mind to teach it to my son as soon as he was old enough to catch flies.

III

The damp heat condemned the Indians to relative inactivity. Their chief occupation consisted of making head-dresses with toucan feathers and chest ornaments with seeds and insects' wings. Was it wisdom on their part, or merely lethargy?

They had no warlike neighbours. The only dances that took place around the hut were those performed by women to ensure the protection of the full moon for the manioc plantation.

I let the days glide by, refusing to disturb either my own peace or the peace enjoyed by my friends. The *musachi*, the Little Bear, moved round the southern sky, marking out our time into periods of unchanging calm.

Then the witch-doctor came, unexpectedly. This lean, lonely devil, who brought up his canoe alongside mine, must have felt it his duty to revive fanaticism among the tribes for one night of drinking and invocation was enough to change the Indians' attitude from friendliness to hostility. In the morning they would not look at me nor speak to me. If I had not demanded food they would have forgotten to give it to me.

I roused myself from my lethargy. It was time to go.

I told the Jivaros and they were unreasonably slow to understand. Yaouen and Tie looked on while I made ready to start. They saw me pack up my bed and carry the bags into the canoe without showing the slightest interest or moving to give me help. When I launched forth on to the current, they watched for a while before returning to their dark hut where the witch-doctor lay resting.

Luckily the river was high, which made the rapids easier to negotiate and I sailed swiftly and smoothly down to the Santiago. Two days later I touched ground near the big hut of the Katirpesa in its quiet glade. Here, among the Huambiza who had taken me on my last trip, a final bargain was struck: for the price of two-score needles, some red thread and some mirrors, two lads agreed to travel south with me.

FIVE : THE GORGE OF MANSERICHE

I

I stood on a beautiful shore on the right bank of the Santiago, opposite its confluence with the Marañon. The two Huambiza Jivaros, who dared not penetrate into Aguaruna territory, were going home. I could still see their canoe far away along the river, but I knew it would be useless to call them back. Instead I looked at the scenery.

It was majestic enough to silence any chatterer. On the right the Marañon opened up, wide and swift, leaping and rolling and roaming from stone to stone. It filled its whole bed, rose above it and then sank back to find it cluttered with tree trunks, moss and sand.

How far it had come! It had begun as a waterfall issuing from a glacial lake of the Cordillera of Huayhuash, 16,000 feet up; it had followed the channels made by erosion, rushed through the frozen zones, lingered for an instant in the calm waters of a mountain lake, passed through the treeless plains as though eager to have done with meagre vegetation and semi-deserts, snatched up streams and then torrents from the eastern and western ranges and tumbled in a few hours down sheer abysses. Now imprisoned in gorges and eating them away as it passed, now free to roll its tons and tons of water over hundreds of miles in a race at a speed which baffles the imagination, it had suddenly come up against an unbroken chain that barred its way and turned it towards the west. Two hundred miles from the Pacific it was condemned to a new and unexpected way of life, only to be attained after passing through the gorge of Manseriche, the most formidable of all its obstacles.

The dark waters of the Santiago, patiently drained from the basins of the Ecuadorean mountains, brought new strength to the Marañon as it prepared to attack the narrow opening 2,000 feet high and barely visible in the wooded wall of rock that rose on its eastern side.

II

I had already passed through this gorge a few weeks before while crossing from the lands of the Aguaruna Indians to those of the Huambizas. It had taken eight hours to travel seven or eight miles; it was a desperate struggle against adverse currents, against eddies, against two or three whirlpools so powerful that they suck up and swallow like blades of grass the tallest forest trees, branches and roots and all. The six men who were with me that day will not easily forget their agonizing strain and sweat. The Indians were terrified of this dark passage, sometimes no more than 40 yards across (when it issues from the gorge, the Marañon is 400 or 500 yards wide). I could sympathize with them.

That day, the Marañon was falling and the pilot stone that stands up in the middle

of the water was fairly well exposed; the weather was fine. We had packed into our long boat all that we needed for the venture: paddles, poles, thick rope and scoops for baling out.

The first few yards, almost before we had left the big masses of rock that protect the Borja station, gave the oarsmen proof of the strength of the water's resistance. The eddies on its surface gave the illusion that it was moving forward in great glaucous patches. It was surprising that as we changed banks we were not carried away several miles, but, by paddling to right and to left, by making use of counter-currents to regain a few yards, by hugging the banks which grew continually steeper, we reached the mouth of the gorge in an hour.

It was dark in that ever-narrowing passage; here and there a slight bend was marked by some rock or by a tree overhanging the void.

It took several minutes to get round the pilot stone and then the fun began. The whirlpools with their rings of foam could be seen from a fair way off. We advanced, paddling vigorously and carefully clinging close to the wall of rock. Suddenly a yawning gap appeared and immediately a counter-current shot us forward to the brink of the whirlpool. On a calm day, as this was, you have to take advantage of the turning movement of the water and right your boat at the crucial moment to change sides. The manoeuvre was successful; it had to be repeated three or four times and was the most thrilling experience of the whole adventure. It is never easy to steer the course of a big canoe to within half an inch, but when one's life depends on that half-inch...

When our craft reached the heart of the gorge, in the spot where the stream rushes headlong between two walls only 40 yards apart, we had to fight inch by inch; but the rhythm of the paddles never slackened. There is nothing more reliable than the human engine.

A red-beaked *pawil*, then a white *garsa*, perched on their branches, watched us pulling away for a long time. We reached a mass of rocks where it was possible to breathe for a moment before hauling the canoe by means of ropes. After that, shipping water in buckets-full, we progressed upstream to the western pilot stone, where the gorge widens out. The line of peaks of the Cordillera of the Andes appeared opposite like a spectacular stage set. We still had three hours of toil before reaching the confluence of the Santiago with the Marañon, though we could see it clearly on our right. The noise made by the Marañon as it rushed over this pebbly floor would have drowned our voices; but in any case the exaltation of our journey upstream had left us bereft of speech.

III

And now I was looking down the river. Behind the dark wall, crowned with great gloomy clouds, stretched out the alluvial plain of the Amazon.

Of the vast desert of trees, lianas and marshes, we had explored only a minute section. Before me lay a journey from east to west across this continent covered by its "sadistic and virginal" forest. From the seething waters of the Manseriche gorge, with their deafening roar, to its mouth in the Bay of Marajo, 14 or 15 miles wide, I was to follow the Amazon day by day.

CONCLUSION

Our journey was over. What had we gained? Turning back to the preliminary report on the expedition, I find it says, unemotionally: "Our itinerary enabled us to visit the three principal tribes of Jivaro Indians, to study the Jivaro tongue and obtain a detailed analysis of the technical, aesthetic and social activities of these tribes, particularly their technical methods of providing and preparing food, hunting, fishing, making clothes and building dwellings, and the process of head-shrinking."

We brought back a collection of objects, gramophone records of incantations, 120 measurement files and the record of a certain number of blood groups selected from among the three Jivaro tribes; and a zoological collection, an ethnographic film and 3,000 photographs.

But we gained more than scientific knowledge. We gained in humanity. We arrived in Jivaro territory armed with such information about the Indians as can be acquired from museums and travellers' accounts. Then came that day I have described when we found ourselves face to face with the Indians themselves. The inhabitants of the hut were watching me, motionless and silent. I had looked forward to this moment as to something that would gratify my pride, but when it came I was overwhelmed by a far stronger emotion; the Indians about whom I had dreamed and read were now living creatures; and in spite of their nakedness, the black locks hanging over their shoulders and their black wooden spears, I saw them as human beings and I smiled at them. Our eyes met, our hands touched; and that was enough to shrivel away like a dead leaf all my patiently acquired erudition.

I had to start learning again – learning about life. Since then, in all the years I have spent in the forest, I have always tried to consider the Indians as men capable of thinking and feeling like others, and I have gone through the forest paths of the Amazon, hunting for signs which would help me to understand and make friends with them. Friendliness towards the Indian seems to me the best "method" for an explorer. Conquerors, colonial settlers and even scientific investigators have too often been lacking in it. And yet it is an essential element in our relations with the men of the forest who, otherwise, withhold their secret from us.

In 1947 a Jivaro called Ti, who had accompanied me into the hostile region of the Huambizas and with whom I had been staying for a few days, gave me a proof of devotion and friendliness such as I have rarely met among the people of his tribe, and which, for an explorer, are not merely satisfying but hold promise of progress and mutual understanding. Ti feared and detested all small-scale settlers of mixed blood and all Indians of his group who had accepted contact with white men. He had got nothing from them save, by a roundabout series of exchanges, one machete and the Spanish word *matar*, to kill. He would never have gone near them had I not been smitten with dysentery and immobilised by the poisonous bite of a tiresome spider. He saw me in such a wretched state that he overcame his repulsion and carried me in his canoe as far as a hut on the Rio Santiago where dwelt a family of Indians wearing trousers (this denotes not intelligence, but a voluntary or involuntary state of civilization). Ti deposited me on the shore and vanished quickly upstream. He had wanted to save my life and had risked his liberty to that end.

Ti, and all men like him who lead self-sufficient lives, are in general considered as "savages". It would be more correct to call them refractory natives. Savages lead an existence strictly limited to the satisfaction of their essential needs and devoid of any cultural element. I doubt whether so low a level of humanity can be found among even the most wretched groups of Indians. Refractory natives are men who do not wish to live in a different way from their ancestors and who therefore reject relations with us. I think this is the case with the Indians, for if we overcome the obstacles that separate us from the free Indian, the forest, the marshland, and still more his mistrust and hostility, we come upon an unsuspected world; the animistic and magical world of the Indians. The customs we think most barbarous, such as the shrinking of human heads, are understandable if seen in their relation to a well organized society which is convinced of its own supernatural origins. There lies the whole secret. The problem is how to get to the sources of these things. The refractory Indians are evidently the only ones who retain in their entirety the techniques, beliefs and legends of their ancestors, and the only ones who can still explain these. But they are suspicious of the white man, and are as ready to mislead him in his researches as to confuse his path in the forest so that he may never reach the glades where they live.

These refractory groups are not very numerous. In my opinion, about 60 per cent. of the whole Indian population, spread over nearly four million square miles of forest, has been adapted or assimilated by our culture. Moreover, more than 30 per cent. of those Indians who live out of touch with civilized people make contact with them from time to time for purposes of barter. There remain, therefore, less than ten per cent. of natives who live completely and voluntarily isolated within the virgin forest. These ten per cent. do not make up autonomous tribes; they are small groups detached from certain tribes. The proportion of refractory natives is not identical in each of these; indeed, in most Amazonian tribes it is non-existent. Among the Yahuas, whom I visited last year, 150 to 200 Indians out of a population of about 3,000 live in isolation.

Among the Chavantes of Brazil or the Jivaros of Ecuador the proportion is far higher. But the average of ten per cent, seems to me valid for the Amazonian region as a whole.

These groups of authentic Indians are rapidly disappearing, firstly because of the continuous advance of pioneers (missionaries, small settlers, military stations, outposts of the Indians' Protective Service) into the interior of the forest, and secondly because the dispersal of the small Indian communities deprives their members of the social structure of the great tribes which formerly ensured their protection. The free Indian is therefore threatened with imminent extinction. If only this elimination of the last centres of a genuinely Indian form of life were compensated by a satisfactory and well-founded integration of the native into our own civilization!

But unfortunately, the inevitable fusion takes place in a way which is painful and sometimes disastrous for the Indian. Who is responsible? Neither the settler nor the missionary; only poverty. The economy of "modern" Amazonia is so rudimentary that it merely domesticates, instead of liberating, the newcomers who venture on to the outskirts of the forest. Moreover, Europeans, throughout the centuries, have acted with singular lack of understanding towards the Indian. At different periods he has served as a butt for irony or a theme for political theorizing, he has satisfied the cult of exoticism or the need for cheap labour; throughout, he has been kept in a sort of "intellectual zoo" and prevented from entering any progressive community. It is time to stop considering the Indian as somebody different from ourselves and incapable of progress; it is time to discard the ridiculous caricatures that delighted us as children. Thus the first false image that must be destroyed is that of the feathered cannibal shooting arrows at the brave traveller armed with a butterfly net... Our contemporaries are still haunted by this concept, just as our forebears were by the legend of El Dorado, the golden kingdom, or the lost cities in the marshlands. We need the element of wonder, granted; but we shall not find it in romantic tales. The wonder lies in the Indians' simple, primitive way of life, in which their thousand-year-old past still retains something of its strength and vitality.

The first duty of those interested in the fate of the Indian should be, it seems to me, to restore to him his human dignity. Then the most refractory and hostile Indians accept contact with us. We shall witness the rapid evolution of blow-gun hunters and harpoon-fishermen; we shall see them learn to use modern tools and to free themselves from their old superstitious terrors. What seemed, only yesterday, an insuperable barrier between us, is seen today to be merely a matter of nuances. And I wonder if the city-dweller and the man of the virgin forest are not, perhaps, closer to one another in the strange world we live in than at any other time – if we are not somehow like them, confronted with the great problems of our day... I know that this is a private and somewhat sentimental opinion! Nevertheless, neither the humiliating condition of the domesticated Indian nor the still puzzling standards of the refractory Indian should mislead us. We have, moreover, one way of realizing the cultural potentialities of the Indian, by looking into the relatively recent past of certain people of the Amazonian region.

A glance at the map will help us to understand. The Amazon and its principal tributaries rise in the Cordillera of the Andes, and these huge rivers appear to be the only travel routes, the only means of migration used during centuries by Indian tribes. When I visited the valley of the Marañon, the upper course of the Amazon, I found traces of tribes which had come out of the forest and had built temples, fortresses and towns in the high regions of the Andes. In 1947, when I went down the Marañon from its source to a spot seven degrees latitude South, I observed, and partly studied, more than thirty groups of ruins of which one, Garo, had been an urban centre of 5,000 inhabitants, perhaps even more. The drawings, the architectural motifs, the pottery, the funeral rites which prove the Amazonian origins of the peoples established on these foothills of the Andes before the Incas, are evidence of a high degree of cultural development in the ancestors of the forest Indians. The Incas, excellent soldiers, road-builders and organizers as they were, only conquered them at a later date. When one knows what store the Incas set on local cultures, which they incorporated into their empire, and to what extent their achievements were based on the learning of their victims, one can judge the importance of the peoples of the Upper Marañon, of Utubamba and neighbouring valleys, which are clearly of Amazonian origin. It matters little that they belonged to one or other of the three great waves of migrants whose traces can be found amongst different tribes in the forest. They were Amazonians. If the forest Indians proved unable to preserve their civilization in the form which we saw in the Andes, it was because of the forest itself, which offers man nothing but wood, sand and mud. In such conditions, mere survival is a proof of intelligence and courage.